THE INSIDE EDGE

THE INSIDE EDGE

High Performance Through Mental Fitness

Peter Jensen, Ph.D.

Performance Coaching Inc.
Rockwood, Ontario
Canada

Excerpts from *Acta Psychologica*, *Coaching Review* and *Golf Digest* reprinted with permission.

Quote from Sylvie Bernier reprinted with permission of the authors from *Psyched: Inner Views of Winning* by Terry Orlick and John Partington.

Canadian Cataloguing in Publication Data

Jensen, Peter Kenneth, 1946-
    The inside edge : high performance through mental fitness

Includes bibliographical references
ISBN 0-7715-9154-3 (bound)   ISBN 0-7715-9026-1 (pbk.)

1. Success in business — Psychological aspects.
2. Success — Psychological aspects. I. Title.

BF637.S8J46 1992   158   C92-094323-3

Cover design by James Jensen, Atom Graphics, Calgary

Performance Coaching Inc.
Rockwood, Ontario, Canada
N0B 2K0 (519) 856-9064

Printed in Canada

To my friend Vanessa Oliver and all children everywhere who day to day show tremendous courage in the face of life's extraordinary challenges.

Contents

FOREWORD

I met Peter Jensen four years ago. I was in the process of planning a manager's meeting for my company, Nesbitt Thomson, and a mutual friend recommended Peter as a dynamic motivational speaker. After our initial meetings I knew that Peter's message was something that would interest my partners. And so began what is now a beneficial business relationship.

Motivational speakers are often like Chinese food. They fill you up with plenty of ideas, but the messages are digested quickly—before you know it you are hungry again. This was certainly not the case with Peter Jensen. The time he spent with that group of managers has proven to be a great investment—one that continues to pay valuable dividends. The major issues and life skills he discussed, all of which are described in *The Inside Edge,* provide us with many simple and useful tools to help us be the best that we can be.

I believe so strongly in the philosophy that Peter imparts that many of the departments within Nesbitt Thomson have been given the opportunity to hear about his ideas, and to learn from them. The publication of this book will mean that a much larger audience will have access to these same ideas and skills.

Peter has become a personal friend and I marvel at his high energy and positive attitude. *The Inside Edge* will now provide me with a constant reminder of the skills I have learned through my association with him.

In reviewing the many aspects of the book—imagery, positivism, self-talk, reframing—I am struck by their common sense. Peter humanizes these apparently esoteric concepts and offers many suggestions for applying their skills to everyday situations.

I am particularly honored to be writing this foreword because of my involvement with the Juvenile Diabetes Foundation Canada. I am deeply indebted to Peter for his volunteer work for the Foundation and for his generosity in donating part of the proceeds from each sale of *The Inside Edge* to funding diabetes research.

Fourteen years ago my eldest daughter, Joanna, developed diabetes; she was five years old. Living with diabetes is not easy. The fear of future complications constantly weighs down upon her, but Joanna chose long ago not to be a victim. She decided to be someone who would live her life to the fullest.

My wife, Bonnie, and I have "reframed" the problem of dealing with a chronic illness. We have focused our energies on supporting the Juvenile Diabetes Foundation Canada, to raise funds in the hope of finding a cure. By using positivism, we have been able to develop a game plan that promotes the ideas of community involvement and caring for others who have health concerns. We have a vision of the future—a world where diabetes does not exist. Peter's philosophy is important to the creation and promotion of that vision.

I am proud to introduce this book to you as a friend, a business associate, a volunteer, and most of all a strong believer in everything *The Inside Edge* represents.

Terry Jackson
Vice-Chairman, Nesbitt Thomson, Inc.
Treasurer, Juvenile Diabetes Foundation International
Past Chairman, Juvenile Diabetes Foundation Canada

FORWARD REVISITED

by Terry Jackson
June 26, 1999

Much has occurred over the last 8 years since I had the
pleasure of writing the initial forward for "The Inside Edge".
The dynamic, frenetic and ever changing times in which we
live points to the importance of managing our time more
successfully. We need to ensure that our lives are balanced
and that we are equipped to meet all of life's challenges.
The principles with which Peter Jensen has enlightened our
minds continue to be as relevant as ever and go a long way
to outfitting us for the future.

Even as my corporate life has moved through Nesbitt
Thomson, Nesbitt Burns and now to the Bank of Montreal,
my co-workers and I have been fortunate to be able to tap
into Peter's thoughts. "The Inside Edge" and Peter's many
seminar and coaching offerings have afforded thousands
the opportunity of learning and self-discovery.

The messages live on, and we are encouraged to revisit and
reconfirm his recommendations regularly.

Executive Vice President
Sales & Marketing
Personal & Commercial Client Group
Bank of Montreal

ACKNOWLEDGMENTS

The vision for this book came from my friend and colleague Bob Wiele. Years ago he saw the potential in applying this material to a broader context than the sports arena in which I was working

Karen Hanley brought my ideas and thoughts to life with a style that smoothed out my rough offerings without turning them into "something that even my mother wouldn't recognize." Her patience, editorial expertise, and sense of humor are marvelous assets. I am very grateful to Karen for all she has done.

Denise Schon and Jackie Rothstein at Macmillan Canada are the ultimate professionals. Their critical eyes, know-how, and blatant cheerleading carried this concept, and a very rough draft, through to the finished product you hold in your hands.

I am also indebted to Vicki Skinner who originally transcribed my meanderings from audiotape to computer disk. Without her patience for my warped sense of humor, we wouldn't have had anything to mould.

The Juvenile Diabetes Foundation Canada team of volunteers and staff brought an energy, enthusiasm, and broader purpose to the book. To Bonnie and Terry Jackson, Karen Mazer, and Hamish Robertson and the whole team, thank you!

To all my teachers past and present I offer my appreciation.

I'm grateful to all the athletes, sports organization, hospitals, medical professionals, patients, corporate executives, corporations, and people I have had the wonderful opportunity to work with. Without them you would be holding 200 blank pages reflecting what I would have known about true, honest, everyday performers.

Finally, the alliteration twins, Shelly Swallow and Sandra Stark, played the key roles in this production. Shelley, my business manager, is a walking and talking character from *The Hitchhiker's Guide to the Galaxy* and a Tom Robbins novel. Her humor, sharp mind, and accounting skills have been the backbone of Performance Coaching Inc.

Sandra Stark's insights and material are everywhere in this book. Her counseling background has brought much depth to the book. Her husband is questionable...or more accurately, he is constantly questioned, challenged, and forced (willingly) to grow. To my wife, Sandra, my love and thanks.

Finally, to you who have purchased this book, I thank you for your trust in me—trust that I have something to offer that you can use—and for your support of the children who face the real challenge in life...life.

Introduction

Nothing endures but change.

—Heraclitus

It was exceptionally warm for February, particularly for Calgary. Normally at this time of the year the snow would have been drifting, and temperatures would have been well below freezing, but a warm wind, a chinook, had blown in and turned the opening of the Calgary Olympics into a mild and springlike day—wonderful for anyone not dressed in the Arctic wear designed for the Canadian team for the marching-in ceremony.

All the athletes and team members had gathered in an arena adjacent to McMahon Stadium, and were getting ready to march the mile route out the back of the arena into the side entrance of the stadium, where 80,000 people waited to greet them. The Americans had started a "wave" in the arena to add spice to the festivities, and I, dressed in my red-and-white Canadian team outfit, joined in.

I work in the area of sports psychology. Now, it might seem strange to you that I would be preparing to march in the opening ceremonies of the Olympic Games, but I was there because I worked with 17 of the Canadian athletes and was living with them in the Olympic village, where, the coaches had decided, I would be better placed to help them. Everyone in the village is considered a member of the team and is given all the paraphernalia that goes with it.

So there I was, about to experience as close as possible what elite athletes experience—the kind of pressure that they deal with. Not only would I be participating in the opening and closing ceremonies, but I would also be working with the athletes at rinkside and a variety of sporting venues during the games themselves. It would be the nearest thing to being inside their skins—almost as if I were out there performing myself. This experiential perspective was going to enhance my understanding of what athletes must deal with, since until then I had relied solely on their attempts to describe their experiences to me. I saw this as a tremendous learning opportunity.

The Calgary games, like every Olympics, will be remembered for some rare moments of triumph—and just as many bitter disappointments. Here were individuals called upon to display maximum concentration and to perform to their highest capabilities under the most demanding and stressful conditions. It was during these games that figure skater Elizabeth Manley pulled off her astonishing silver-medal performance, and Brian Boitano prevailed over Brian Orser for the gold. We flew with the Jamaican bobsled team and soared with ski jumper Eddie the Eagle. It was also at Calgary that speed skater Dan Jansen, following the death of his sister, tumbled to defeat not just once, but in two races, and warm winds delayed ski-jumping and bobsledding events day after day, causing athletes to lose the edge that they had trained months to achieve.

There have been many Olympic Games since Calgary. What I learned in Calgary, Albertville, Atlanta and Sydney and in preparing athletes for Seoul, Barcelona, Lillehammer, Nagano and Salt Lake City (I didn't travel with the Olympic teams to these games) has truly been an advanced education, one I value as highly as my academic training. I am currently working with the Canadian Synchronized

Swimming team preparing for the 2004 games in Athens. Since 1988 I have also worked with hundreds of corporations and have learned a great deal about that high-performance environment, as well. Of the many things that I have found in common in the arenas of sports and business, most notable to me are the inner skills—the mental fitness, if you will—required by those who wish to perform at a higher level. I have also found the same skills operative in cancer patients and in other people faced with incredible challenges in their lives. This book presents the skills that I have learned from my work with these high-level performers in sports, business, and health.

Choosing a major thrust for the book was particularly difficult because of the unique combination of my experiences. Should I gear it to athletes? Should it be a business book or a health book? At the same time, I wanted it to be a personal book. Upon reflection, I realized the common thread running through all I do and who I am is the importance of training from the inside out, of developing psychological skills that enhance performance. These skills are universally applicable to any situation where pressure and the need for excellence are equally present—be it healing yourself, dealing with a deadline, skating in a world championship, or mastering a new skill. We constantly attribute failure or success in our careers and personal lives to the inner dimension, to what goes on inside of us: "I didn't have enough confidence"; "I got too nervous"; "I couldn't control my anger"; "I felt so good"; "I told myself it's now or never." Yet rarely do we consciously work on developing and training our inner potential. Why has such a powerful and pervasive aspect of performance systematically been underplayed and overlooked in our culture?

As we look at the direction in which our society is moving, the future appears to hold constant change and increasing complexity. Economically we are struggling as our major institutions make the transition from the Industrial Age to the Information Age and to a new world order. It is an exciting time fraught with challenge. Businesses, caught in this changing landscape, maintain their quest for constant improvement and increased profits. More and more emphasis is placed on innovation, productivity, customer service, and flexibility. All these changes, and their accompanying demands to adjust, have a major impact on our inner worlds.

We can now say with certainty that thoughts, feelings, and imagination have a profound influence on performance. What was once fringe is becoming mainstream; what was once stigmatized is now lauded as essential. Out of necessity, perhaps, but also to benefit health and personal development, we are ready to take a step inward in order to move forward. John Welch, former chief executive officer of General Electric Inc., in an article in *Fortune* magazine said: "If we are to get the reflexes and speed we need, we've got to simplify and delegate more—simply trust more. We need to drive self-confidence deep into the organization. A company can't distribute self-confidence, but it can foster it by removing layers and giving people a chance to win."

In a seven-year study of 200 Illinois Bell executives following the deregulation of the telephone industry in the United States, psychologists Suzanne Kobasa and Salvatore Maddi found that half the group developed chronic stress symptoms and became ill, while the other half survived that trying period without suffering significant illness or symptoms of stress. What made the difference? The major factor that distinguished those who thrived and moved forward from those who got sick and suffered a drop in their performance was what Maddi and Kobasa called personality "hardiness." In their book, *The Hardy Executive: Health Under Stress*, they identified three characteristics of a hardy personality: control, commitment, and challenge.

Executives with hardy personalities found some aspect of difficult situations that they could control—whether it was taking action or choosing to avoid getting uptight when they were unable to influence the outcome. They chose transformational, as opposed to regressive, coping. Managers who got sick or who sank to low performance displayed a sense of alienation; they felt externally controlled, often overwhelmed or helpless, and tried to find security by regressing and turning situations back to the way they were.

Hardy executives felt they had a mission and got highly involved to make things happen. Their sense of purpose and active involvement helped to minimize the threat of stressful conditions and provided a basis for coping with problems and setbacks. Commitment, of course, also helped to get the job done. Those who were committed felt less stress because they believed in their ability to transform situations and respond flexibly—to be effective. Those with low hardiness were often bored, unable to find meaning or interest in their lives.

The third variable, challenge, was important because it allowed a positive orientation, a spirit of adventure, a willingness to explore and readjust. The hardy personalities perceived change and stressful life events as positive, creative challenges instead of problems. Those with low hardiness felt threatened by change and uncertainty. The key discovery of this study, and of many others like it, was that the factors contributing to health and sickness had to do with the internal world: perspective, attitude, and personal power. High performance and health are inside jobs.

Rules of the pool

This is not a book of clichés or cute tips, or one of deep philosophical concepts. It is profound only insomuch as you, the reader, gain an awareness or uncover a skill that moves you to where you want to be. This book is for you. Decide how the material feels to you. This is not a book that tells you "you should." When people use the word "should," not only are they suggesting that you aren't doing something, they are saying that you ought to feel guilty about the apparent inadequacy. "Should" is a double whammy: not doing it and feeling guilty. "I really should lose weight." Not only do I not lose the weight, but I also feel guilty about it. I have a sport shirt with a motto that reads: Don't Should on Me.

I'm asking you to be selfish: read this for yourself. Most of us listen with ears for others: "My eldest child might like to read this"; "My boss needs this"; "My wife or husband could use that." Please try to see, listen, and feel in relation to yourself. Once again, I want this book to be personal: changing, winning, healing are all things we do for ourselves.

Having said that, I should also say some of what you read in this book will be right for you, while other information may not strike you as relevant. Let it go. What I'm giving you is what a professor of mine, Alan Affleck, used to call *quid*. If you look up "quid" in the dictionary, it means something to be chewed. No mention is made of whether you are to swallow it. If you don't like the taste of my information, spit it out. Maybe the next course will be more to your liking. Learning resides, after all, in the learner, not in the teacher. You know what's right for you. You make all the choices; you make all the calls. I repeat—this book is for you.

I get carried away with personal enthusiasm for this material from time to time. Please remember, it's all quid. It may sound as though I'm trying to sell you something—perhaps I am. Someone once said, "Whenever two people are talking, one of them is selling."

What am I trying to sell to you? My goal is to wake up the observer in all of you so that you can seize control, gain confidence, and face commitment in challenging situations (a.k.a. life). I'm not suggesting that you suddenly make radical changes; the elite athletes I work with don't make major adjustments to their mental approaches instantly. They make what Buckminster Fuller called "trim-tab adjustments"—small changes that result in major changes down the road. Imagine if the *Titanic* had made a trim-tab adjustment of 10 degrees south when it had left England. That's right! No billion dollar movie and it might have ended up in the Bermuda Triangle and perhaps another story and another movie.

I want to provide you with a way of understanding how what goes on inside you has an impact on your performance and your health, and to teach you some skills that will help you access all of your abilities in each of your performance arenas. I hope that when you've finished this book, your perception and awareness will have changed, and that you will hear and see yourself and others differently...you will hear how frequently we all make reference to the inner dimension. As Yogi Berra said, "Sport is 90 percent mental, and the other half is physical". Yogi may not have been much of a mathematician, but he got one thing right: the only reality is the inner one.

CHAPTER ONE

The Inner Dimension

*In every situation, there is a possibility
of improvement; in every life the hidden
capacity for something better. True realism
involves a dual vision, both sight and
insight.*

　　　　　　　　　　　—Lester B. Pearson

Western culture has traditionally placed a high value on logic and the intellect—the ability to retain knowledge, to comprehend, to analyze, to plan. The focus has always been how to translate this kind of thinking into action. This emphasis has served us well. Relatively speaking, we're a successful and affluent society.

There are other facets to the inner dimension, however, that have gone unnoticed; they have been undervalued and thus remain underdeveloped. At best, aspects of our psyche such as intuition, emotion, imagination, suggestibility, spirituality, and how they translate into action have been largely ignored by mainstream culture. More often they have been stigmatized and banished to the realms of psychology, religion, or worse yet, New Age, where the dysfunctional and out of step can dither.

But there is an exciting shift occurring, and that shift is inward to a new frontier—to explore and consider all facets of the inner dimension and how these bearers of wisdom play upon one's actions. This shift has resulted as high performers from the fields of science, medicine, sport, and philosophy try to understand and explain phenomena such as the placebo effect, peak performance, spontaneous remission, survival under impossible conditions, and transformational experiences. As they have searched for explanations, they have discovered that these phenomena are related directly to what people do inside themselves. The search is on to understand and articulate exactly what it is that high performers "do" internally, so that these skills can be taught to *all* who perform in today's complex and competitive world.

Concurrently, a tremendous amount of research is being conducted on the brain. We've all heard it before, but as you read the following statement, I want you to let it sink in and reverberate within you for a few minutes: we are using only five to 10 percent of our brain. What do you suppose the other 90 percent is for? The theory exists that we have many programs waiting to be discovered in our brains; we just don't have the role models yet. For example, we are programmed to learn to speak. Once we have role models—that is, people who can speak—that program will unfold at its correct time without prompting. Are there other programs? Do other role models exist and we just haven't been paying attention? Well, perhaps by studying high performers, people who push themselves beyond what we consider "normal," we can glimpse what they do inside themselves that allows them to be extraordinary. It has always been assumed that these people were smarter, more talented, or worked harder. That may be true, but they also possess inner skills that allow them to "get out" more of what they are capable of. They use their inner resources to a much greater degree than most of us. They have learned to use more of, or make better use of, the power that lies within them, the power of the inside edge.

Who hasn't been in a trying situation—perhaps an emergency with one of our children—where we moved to a place of incredible calm and we dealt with the crisis effectively, then afterward got all nervous and shaken up. Where did we go? Did we suddenly acquire coping skills out of the collective unconscious? Did they suddenly appear out of the sky?

No, we had those capabilities within us.

I recall an exchange in a recent interview with Natan Sharansky, the Soviet dissident who was released from a Soviet concentration camp after nine horrific years of incarceration. The interviewer asked, "How did you survive in such an awful place? How did you stand the deprivations and the beatings?" And Sharansky replied, "I didn't live in their world. I created a world in my mind where I was free... Every person has unlimited resources of resistance." He was then asked, "But how did you stand all that you were faced with, all the negativity and the abuse?" And he replied, "I had to treat them [the guards] just like the weather." In other words, he looked at them as something over which he had no control—somedays it rains, and somedays it's very beautiful. Most days it's pretty neutral. This is the ultimate high-performance, high-health mind-set: finding some controllable aspect of a situation—in this case your perceptions of an experience—and acting on it.

Dr. Herbert Benson, of the Harvard Medical School, brought together the world-champion relaxers: the transcendental meditation (TM) specialists and the Buddhist monks, the progressive-relaxation specialists and the autogenic-training experts (relaxation by suggestion) and possibly people from the post office. He hooked them up to biofeedback equipment to track where they went in deep meditative states. He discovered that in profoundly relaxed states oxygen consumption is dramatically reduced, blood pressure is lowered, heart rate decreases, and alpha waves (brain waves) increase. He found the same patterns in all of his meditation subjects; they all went to the same place physiologically when relaxed. The great irony is that people search the world over for tranquility, and the most peaceful place in the world actually exists within each of us!

There are many more accounts in the media and in books of extraordinary people attributing their success, or failures, to the inner dimension. Leonard Cerullo, a well-known American brain surgeon, was asked by an interviewer, "How do you prepare for the gruelling 10-hour operations that you perform routinely?" He replied by talking about a reading ritual he has at night when he goes to bed. Then he added, "I often wake up in the middle of the night and mentally rehearse upcoming operations. Not only do I rehearse what I normally do, but I imagine things that could go wrong— things that have never happened before—and I see how I will handle them." Ingemar Stenmark, one of the world's great slalom skiers, would often train using only two gates. When asked why, he said, "There is a left turn and right turn—the rest I can do in my mind." It is my hope that after reading this book, you will be more aware of the importance of the inner dimension, and therefore feel motivated to pay attention to and honor your own inner wisdom.

The menu, the model

This book will offer some common-sense lessons from peo- ple who are doing extraordinary things. It will provide you with skills that are applicable to a variety of situations. They are simple, generic, portable skills—trim-tab adjustments, if you will—that you can use every day to improve your moment-to-moment performance and at the same time build a solid foundation for long-term health and physical well-being. They are designed to help you access what you are innately capable of. We're going to discuss six areas, which we will then break down into learnable skills:

- positivism
- active awareness
- energy management
- attentional skills
- imagery
- visioneering

The inner games or skills will allow us to make transitions from poor performance, which is rooted in a confused, anxious, or angry inner state, to an inner world that allows us to access our skills and perform at a higher level in our outside world. Once we have covered all six areas, we will look at the concept of mental preparation and ways to combine the skills we've acquired into a regimen of messages and images that will strengthen us at critical moments in our lives.

These six areas are totally interrelated, so we really could start anywhere, or I could discuss them in any sequence. Many people would argue that I should start with visioneering, because until you know where you're going, how will you know what to do? Others would argue that without awareness we can't take any action. Still others would say attitude is the key, so let's start with positivism. The chapter headings exist to break the material down into bite-sized pieces, but the truth is the information is an integrated whole. You can no more discuss one of these concepts in isolation and derive meaning from it than you can discuss the ingredients of a recipe individually and convey the end result. You can't talk about the ingredients without reference to the whole because when they are combined they add elements to each other, they change each other's nature, and that results in a whole that is completely different from its individual parts. So, for the sake of clarity, we'll talk about the ingredients as separate, distinct entities, but remember that they are not as powerful or as flavorful as when they are combined to produce the whole. And the whole, of course, is you and your life.

The mental condition for high performance doesn't come overnight. I encourage you to take one area, one skill, at a time. Add it to your life and then begin practising another. I counsel an athlete on the women's professional golf tour. When she finds that she is putting too much pressure on herself about a particular shot, she steps back from the ball, mentally goes 2,000 metres high above the golf course, and imagines the golf course as it's laid out on the score card.

She sees that making this shot is just one of 72 or 74 things that she's going to do that day. She gets perspective by backing up, seeing the whole game, and recognizing that this one shot is just a small part of it. So, too, do you need to maintain perspective when learning new skills. All of us are always working on improving something. We can't improve everything all at once. If we put unrealistic expectations on ourselves, we will sabotage our growth by increasing the pressure to be perfect and consequently minimize the opportunities to succeed.

CHAPTER TWO

The Inside Edge

*Avoiding danger is no safer in the long run
than outright exposure. The fearful are
caught as often as the bold.*
                                            —Helen Keller

Some observers say that Jack Nicklaus plays golf almost in a trance, a quiet "no-thought" state in which he, the club, and the ball are one, in which absolute concentration allows him to intuit what to do. He doesn't try to make things happen; he just lets them happen. That concentration isn't a strain—it's a kind of meditation. In such moments of peak clarity Nicklaus visualizes the shot, and—click—it's good.

That kind of mental calm under pressure is foreign to most of us. At times of stress, it's incredible how noisy our heads are inside. All those conflicting thoughts forbidding us to slow down and get on with the job at hand. As speed skater Gaetan Boucher, winner of two Olympic gold medals, said, "During the last 10 minutes, if I start to think about my placement or my opponent, it's all over."

Those who have an inside edge on high performance have mastered the art of mental self-control under pressure. Like Gaetan Boucher, most of us know what to do externally to excel. Our difficulties lie more with getting anxious and upset before an event. Those who consistently answer challenge with their personal best have learned to reprogram their mind-set and arousal level when they get off track. They cope with distractions, let go of undesired responses, calm their minds, and maximize their physical energy. They become their own "head" coaches.

What follow are the stories of four ordinary people who applied mental-fitness skills to their world. The inner-world skills that allowed them to move forward and excel are the subject of the rest of this book. But let's start by examining the results of those who chose, when faced with challenge, to become aware and act in the inner dimension to dramatically improve their outer performance.

The healer

The greatest barrier to harnessing our inner resources on behalf of our own health is what we commonly call "conventional wisdom." We truly believe that healing is something that doctors do for us, as opposed to something that we marshal within ourselves. Yet the role of the inner dimension in healing is well documented. Some of the more dramatic studies point to a relationship between personality type and certain types of diseases. Dr. Martin Seligman, for example, of the University of Pennsylvania, has uncovered a link between what he calls "learned helplessness" and cancer; and the hostility factor in Type-A behavior has been closely linked to heart disease.

Some brave individuals have chosen the path toward self-responsibility in health. I recently had a call from a doctor who is involved with an organization that does health assessments for more than 5,000 corporate executives every year. The doctor had attended a lecture I had given to health professionals entitled "Your Head and Your Health," which examined the mental dimension in personal health and well-being, a subject that we will touch on repeatedly in this book. She wanted to know if I could recommend some resources that might assist the CEO of a large oil company who had cancer. She assured me that the CEO was doing extremely well and knew almost as much about his illness as she did. He had empowered himself by making a commitment, taking some control, and feeling challenged by his illness.

There are many others like this executive. Every day that I lecture, at least one person who is dealing with a serious disease (most frequently cancer) tells me his or her story. I am amazed at the common ground in all of the stories: these people have all begun to take an active role in dealing with their illness.

Dr. Bernie Siegel, author of *Love, Medicine and Miracles*, refers to cancer as a giant wake-up call. I did a workshop for a group of people who are employed in the social-services field, a high-pressure, expanding sector during these tough economic times. Debby Rudack was the cancer patient who approached me that day. She'd not only heard the wake-up call, she'd hit the ground running and has not stopped acting on her own behalf since:

I knew something was wrong for 10 years. I'd have severe stomach cramps and throw up. I lived on aspirin. Finally, in December of 1989, I was diagnosed with cancer. Not any of the types you've heard of before, but a rare kind called mesothelioma, which is asbestos-related and normally attacks the lining of the lungs of old people. It's referred to as an "old man's disease." Well, I'm 36 and a woman, and I got it in the peritoneal cavity.

I was hyper at that time, a typical Type-A and an exercise fanatic, with a full-time job and two part-time ones. I had my son living with me and I was commuting on weekends to my fiancé's, since he lived 300 miles away. I was told that I had a spastic bowel and needed to get help with my personal problems. That may have been true, but my problems turned out to be a lot more than mental. I spent a month in hospital undergoing every examination known to man. A laparotomy revealed the cancer. I had a hysterectomy, six months of chemotherapy and was off work for a year. The longest sur-

vival rate for this type of cancer is seven years.

When I learned about the cancer, naturally I was depressed and cried. I called a friend and talked half the night. After that, I was fine. I thought, that's over—let's go on. Ignorance is bliss. What I don't want to know, I don't have to know. When I'm ready, I can handle it. I just put my time to its best use. I don't see obstacles, just opportunities. There are no more should-haves or what-ifs.

I've gone back to school to work on my master's in social work. My goal is to get into family-law mediation, or counseling, perhaps with cancer patients. I've even thought of getting my doctorate and teaching. What have I got to lose? The image I have of myself that keeps me going is of standing in front of a class teaching. I can see myself so vividly. Then all the garbage of life gets sorted aside.

I just go day to day. I still have two tumors, one on my diaphragm, which can't be removed, and one on my bowel. Neither is traveling nor enlarging. If I had the bowel tumor removed, I'd have to wear a colostomy bag. Every three months I have a checkup, and everyone at the clinic seems surprised to see me back again.

I used imagery when I was undergoing chemotherapy. Unfortunately, the chemo didn't work, so I made a personal decision not to undergo further treatment. Now I use imagery daily to allow myself the peace to refocus and discover what is really going on. If I get strung out or overloaded, it tends to be with the job (for six years, I've been a social-service worker, dealing with welfare, mothers' allowance, and family benefits). And I still tend to worry about other people too much.

In my imagery, I see a tunnel where nothing else is allowed in. As I pass through the tunnel, there are chambers where I stop. They are like portals where I look out and see things from my past—mistakes or things that were not very pleasant. I look at them, acknowledge and accept them, and take whatever responsibility is mine. Then I move on. I'm like anybody else. I still have monkeys on my back. My son has had to go and live with his father, and I'm no longer engaged.

*But I look on my disease as a blessing. It has been the cata-
lyst allowing me to do things I would never have done. I went
on an Outward Bound trip for cancer patients, and that experience has shown me what I am capable of doing. It inspired
me to try sky diving. I went on a trip to Nepal. My affirmation
is: "I don't have time to waste on little things."*

The manager

Managing the inner world to manage the outer world
involves awareness and understanding of the inner dimension, empathy for others, and vision. Gordon Bullock is the
publisher of the 140-year-old *Hamilton Spectator* and chairman of the board of Canadian Press. When he attended my
two-day mental-training workshop, he had just seen his
company through a transitional period in which more than
30 long-term employees had to take an early retirement
because of the recession.

*It was tough for me, not only as a manager but as a per-
son, to see all those people through early retirement. A great
many of them represented long-standing relationships, and
the old familiar faces were no longer a part of my daily existence. I thought the seminar would help me keep up to date
with new methods and keep my energy and mental health
high. I also thought I could pass along some of the skills to the
people I work with to help them deal with the realities of the
times. This is a high-pressure business. The stress is relentless. You either get to it, or it gets to you.*

*I was familiar with the fact that the benefits of deep relax-
ation have been validated medically, but to be able to practice it in an instructional setting was a revelation. I now do it
regularly at home. Other techniques, such as reframing to
gain perspective, or centering to calm down, are valuable at a
time when nothing seems to be going right in business. It
helps to be able to control emotional responses when they
need to be controlled.*

Basically I'm an upbeat person. If I tend to overload, it's under the pressure of the job. And when you're under stress, you think less. Using simple mental techniques helps monitor that arousal level. It's very useful for turning down the heat. The end of a hard, pressure-filled day is the likeliest time for family tensions to occur. You're expected to be as calm as a prophet, but someone says the wrong thing and boom!— you're off. Deep relaxation has helped me to deal better with my two teens at home. It's helped me to deal with their behavior, but not confuse what they do with their worth as children. I now try to prepare for home by mentally dropping the work persona and putting on the persona of husband and father before I actually get home from work.

The balancer: worker/family member/ homemaker

I often use an instrument called the stress-map in my workshops to help people identify the pressures that are affecting them. On occasion I take all the stress-map scores of employees of a particular organization and develop a group profile, thereby identifying that organization's training needs. For example, if the whole organization scores low on compassion or time management, clearly something at the organizational level needs to be changed.

I was working with a large insurance company when I was asked to divide the group into men and women to see if there were any gender differences in stress-map profiles. Contrary to what you might expect in our male-centered society, the women, generally speaking, showed a lot more stress than the men. Within the North American culture, we know that women live longer than men, so it's unlikely that women deal less effectively with stress than men do. When we examined this phenomenon, it became clear that it had to do with two important factors: first, women appear to be more in touch with what is going on inside them and more willing to express their feelings; and second, like it or not, even if the male in the family takes on some household tasks, most frequently it is the woman who is left with the burden of balancing home and work life.

Nevertheless, a good many men ask me how to achieve this difficult balance. Robert Smith, the manager of a large chemical processing plant, is one person who hasn't just made faint gestures. He has turned his life around:

I was on a holiday when I first noticed (or at least chose to acknowledge) that I wasn't doing a very good job of balancing my home and work life. Like most businessmen, I got a tremendous amount of satisfaction, despite the pressure and vast number of changes that were occurring in my organization, from my work world. Goals and objectives are clear, and when you achieve something in the work world it's rewarded almost instantly, or at least the reward is obvious.

One of my three children commented as we were walking down the beach that it was really nice to have me around for a change and to spend time with me.

"We never get to talk, Dad.   We never do anything," he said.

I started to object, feeling a little defensive. "What do you mean, we never...why, just last week, didn't we throw a ball around?"

"No, Dad, that wasn't last week. That was three weeks ago."

Three weeks ago, I thought. I began to observe how much time I spent in my inner world dealing with work-related material. There was a tremendous management inequity. About 90 percent of my skills were applied to my work and, at best, 10 percent to home life. I observed that I was much better at listening and giving people time in my work world than I was at home. The pressures from work had begun to invade my home life. Even before I left the house in the morning, I was already mentally at work, and I was still mentally at work when I arrived home in the evening.

Once I became aware of the imbalance in my life, I was able to use some of the skills that I had learned in a mental-fitness workshop. The balance certainly isn't perfect, but I've come a long way. One of the simple things I do may sound rather silly, but it works. On the way home from work, I pass a shopping center. I have a rule: when I see the shopping center, I imagine the door of my office slamming shut, and I switch my imagery and attention forward to my home—where I am going and what everyone in my house has gone through that day—so that when I arrive home I have already been there mentally for five or ten minutes. On two occasions, I wasn't able to focus on this image, so I pulled my car into the parking lot of the shopping center and sat there until I could let go of what I was doing at work and turn my mental attention to my family.

The other evening I caught myself thinking about work as I was distractedly playing a game with my youngest daughter. She asked me a question, but I didn't catch all of it and I noticed that I was thinking about a problem I was having at work. I excused myself for a minute under the guise of going to the bathroom. I thought, why is that bothering me so much? I realized that I had to do something about the problem, but not at the cost of being a low-performing parent. I made a decision to go back to the office at 9:30 and deal with it, thereby freeing myself to be a parent until the children were in bed. By expressing this clearly to my wife, I was also able to go back to the office in the evening without the guilt I usually felt. It's often as if I am escaping the noisy environment of the house for the quiet, safe, more predictable environment of my office world.

The athlete

The world of athletics is particularly suited to the application of mental skills. Many athletes, from Jack Nicklaus and Johnny Miller to Jean-Claude Killy and Kurt Gibson, acknowledge using mental preparation to perform better.

Sport is a wonderfully clean laboratory; if you change something you can instantly see whether it works, because performance in sport is so easily measured. The pole vaulter can tell you within half a centimeter how his day is going. Most of us don't have that clarity in our lives.

In the early days of the Indianapolis 500, many automobile manufacturers learned lessons under the intense heat of world-class competition that have been applied for decades to the everyday automobile. In the same way, we can examine some of the inner skills that differentiate world champions from also-rans. According to Canadian decathlete Michael Smith, who set a personal best, broke the Canadian record, and won the silver medal at the world championships in Tokyo in 1991, "Most athletes have done all the physical work they need to do to prepare themselves. So when it comes down to it, I'd say close to 90 percent of it is mental."

A computer-generated banner, hastily taped by students to a window at New College at the University of Toronto, reads "We're Proud of Micheal Smith". Well they might be. The decathlon, two days of 10 events, ranging from discus and javelin, to high jump and pole vault, to 100-, 400-, and 1,500-metre races, arguably decides the world's best athlete. After Tokyo, Smith was ranked as the second best athlete in the world.

Smith, 24, six foot five and 217 pounds, epitomizes inner balance. This quality is the essential survival tool for the decathlon, which more than any sport requires a balance of skills, physical and mental. It takes power to put a shot 15.5 meters, agility to clear the bar in the pole vault, and speed to burst to the finish in the 110-metre hurdles. It's a sport that is a blend of power with no bulk, speed with technique.

The son of a nurse and a high school teacher, who grew up in Kenora, Ontario, Michael also has a balanced attitude to competition. "People think it's incredible to set world records, but at the same time, it's easy to be humbled by someone who's fighting a personal battle, be it medical or psychiatric. I have to throw a javelin, for example. What's that compared with fighting cancer?"

This perspective led him to sacrifice some points to help U.S. decathlete Dan O'Brien take the gold at Tokyo. "It was the last event, and I couldn't catch him. He had a 300-point lead. In the decathlon, everyone has his strengths and weaknesses. We're not competing against each other so much as against the tape measure and the clock. I'm better at the 1,500-metre than he is, and he had a chance to break the world record, so I asked him if he wanted me to pace him in the 1,500-metre race."

To compete with the world's best and at the same time be able to keep that kind of mental balance is Smith's greatest strength. It's instructive to hear him describe how he prepares for competition:

I don't put numbers on myself. I just go out looking to perform the best I can technically. The distances and times take care of themselves. If I say I want to hit 16 metres, for example, it's the wrong approach for me. I have to think of my body, not of the end result. Even at the Olympics, I'm committed to the same approach—to try to achieve my personal best. In the stadium, there's no one else helping you. You're all alone. The only person you really have to answer to is yourself.

The night before, and also the night between the two days of events, I have to get a good night's sleep. That's where deep relaxation and breathing techniques come in. Sometimes it's really hard to come down. The day of the event, the main thing is that I need to stay relaxed. I can't afford to waste any energy over two days of events. I get up about four or five hours before the start of the event—5:00 a.m. at the latest. I know my body, and it takes that long to get into the right rhythm. I approach the day casually, like any other day, and have a normal warm-up away from the track. I begin to get into my competition mind-set once I'm at the track, about two and a half hours before the first start. I have a slow, easy warm-up there and begin to think about what I want to achieve. I use imagery constantly—it's no longer a conscious effort—picturing myself as if I'm on a video screen. I picture each event before I do it.

At a major meet, we're down by the track about 45 minutes before the start. I concentrate on staying warm, and that's when I really begin to get into the competitive state. I'm aware of all the people around. There are 50,000 people in the stands, and you're surrounded by the best guys in the world. If you lose your focus, it's easy not to regain it. I need to stay focused on what I need to do as an individual. In keeping focus, I almost go on automatic pilot. I use breathing and pos-itive self-talk, saying things to myself like "I'm ready. Let's have a good time." I go into each event looking to have fun, even if it is world-class competition. I allow in only positive thoughts. The negative can creep in, especially if I'm recover-ing from an injury. But you just look at it as another obstacle. Accept it. Work on other strengths. Focus on the positive, even if there is a negative aspect.

During the last five minutes, I need to achieve a certain aggression level. The adrenaline starts to flow. In the first event, the 100-metre, for example, you've got to have hair-trigger reaction time. It's all over in 10 seconds. I have to change my mind-set for every event. The second event is the long jump, where you have three attempts. You can't stay up between each attempt, or you'll burn out your energy. When I'm not jumping, I'm relaxed. When I'm down to two guys ahead of me, I start thinking about the jump. When I'm down to the last guy, I'm ready. I'm on the runway, centered and focused, before he's off. Once the event is done, it's history, whether I did well or not. You let it go, even if it's great. Sometimes if you've really had a great performance it's a big-ger distraction. People come up to you and say, "Wow, you're really hot!" It's hard to get back to where you need to be for the next event.

I have a different energy-management scale for every event. The 100-metre and 110-metre hurdles need to be at maximum arousal level—a 10. The others that have a techni-

cal aspect—for example, the throws—need to be at about a seven or eight. You can't be wild and too pumped up where skill is involved. Different attentional styles are also required. For the technical events, such as the pole vault, you need to be narrow and internal. You need to feel through the event from the inside, not from the outside in. The 1,500-meter needs you to be a bit more external to be aware of other guys jostling for position, for example. If I overload, it can be in paying attention to other competitors or getting overexcited by the crowd. You have to use the crowd, but you can't lose yourself in it.

Sport cascades into the rest of my life. I've been training since the fall of 1985. I didn't have Olympic expectations then; I just let things progress. That seems to be the best approach for me. I use the same approach, whether in sport, business, or relationships. Beyond the Olympics, I don't have concrete plans for the future. I just think of success and keep a successful attitude. Success is 99 percent preparation. If you set yourself up for winning, rarely will you fail.

Getting out your own best performance

Over the next 100 or so pages you can expect to become more aware of what goes on inside you and how that can interfere with or enhance your performance. You can expect to be asked to reflect about the way you approach your world—the mind-sets and mind traps that dictate the way you live your life. You can expect to be challenged, but to have fun, too, because this book is intended as a playful exercise.

But you will also learn those skills that Debby Rudack, Gordon Bullock, Robert Smith, and Michael Smith have put to use so successfully. You will understand how to narrow your attentional focus to concentrate more fully on a particular task, how to relax with the aid of the centering technique, and how to use imagery to enhance your performance.

Success will not come from changes in the way your company, for example, operates or is organized, it will come from acquiring a mental edge to perform in difficult circumstances. When a performer—athlete, business person, or anyone waging a difficult personal battle—enters a high-performance state, he or she is relaxed, yet at the same time totally concentrated and energized. The skills of the champion's mind-set are the skills that will drive those who will excel in the workplace and in their personal lives.

CHAPTER THREE

Positivism

*Blessed is he who expects nothing, for he
shall never be disappointed*
—Alexander Pope

Mother Teresa did not walk through the ghettos of Calcutta "awfulizing"—saying, "This is awful. That is terrible. There's nothing we can do." She was not paralyzed into inactivity. Neither are an aunt and uncle of mine who have lost both their children. It has been difficult for them over the past few years, but I can tell you without question that were you to meet them, you'd be impressed. You would find them likable and positive. You would see that they have tremendous sadness about them on occasion—that is their reality—but you would also see the wonderful, warm, positive attitude that they have chosen to maintain. They have not been paralyzed by the disasters that they have been faced with in their lives.

Lots of things happen to us that aren't very pleasant, from small things such as getting a traffic ticket, to life's ultimate sorrows. But we have a choice in how we deal with them—the choice between prosperity consciousness and poverty consciousness. Prosperity-conscious people expect good things to happen and see setbacks as temporary circumstances. Poverty-conscious people expect problems to occur—setbacks are the norm. To these people, positive occurrences are temporary and will be paid for "in spades" later. Some poverty-conscious people are pessimists (a pessimist is a person who, when faced with two awful alternatives, chooses both of them); worry, doubt, and fear are their primary reactions to the world. Every group or family has a professional worrier. My retired neighbor, Ian, is a classic case. "What a wonderful day," I said to him late last fall. "We'll pay for it this winter" was his quick reply.

People aren't born this way; they learn it. Many of us were brought up in families where this kind of thinking was the norm; our parents themselves may have been brought up this way. Poverty consciousness is frequently cross-generational and is shaped by societal events and attitudes, both of which are beyond the scope of any one person's control. The skill is to notice when we have adopted such a worldview and consciously choose to change that response to life.

Another example of poverty-conscious people are the ones who, when you encounter them, never leave you feeling as good afterward as you did before they walked through the door. They view the world from the stance of a victim; their general refrain is "You won't believe what they're doing to me now." They constantly see the locus of control as being outside themselves. They engage in what I call *opticalrectumitis*, which translates loosely as "having a shitty outlook on life." If they're in a bar at about five to four in the afternoon, the waiter or waitress walks over and says, "Excuse me, you'll have to leave now. We'd like to start the happy hour."

One of the most critical things that we have to recognize about being positive—or prosperity conscious—is that it does not necessarily mean being happy. Some of the most positive events in our lives haven't been any fun at all. We have all lived through tough circumstances that have helped get us to where we are now; that is to say, how we dealt with those situations was critical to our growth and development.

When we look back, however, no matter how important such events were as growth experiences, we never want to go through them again.

Many companies, like people, are poverty conscious in that they limit their vision to a narrow perspective. IBM, for example, defined itself as a communications company, rather than a maker of typewriters, during the Second World War. Other companies, which were as well positioned as IBM, insisted that they were in the business of making type-writers and could not marshal the government resources to assist them that IBM did.

Opportunity presents itself in strange ways, but we have to be willing to recognize it—even when it's wearing camou-flage. Take the British condom manufacturer whom in one of the more ingenious examples of prosperity consciousness I have ever heard of, made a (financial) killing during the Gulf War. After reading that soldiers were having difficulty keeping sand out of their rifle barrels in the desert, he sold 500,000 condoms—in camouflage pattern—to the coalition forces to place over the ends of their rifles during sand-storms.

Five years ago I approached a major North American cor-poration with an eye to conducting some stress-manage-ment workshops. "Oh, no," I was told, "we don't use the word 'stress' here. People will think something's wrong or that the workplace causes stress." With a new CEO at its head, the same organization contacted me three years later and asked me to conduct the workshops and call the pro-gram "stress management": "We want people to become familiar with that word and learn how to deal with what goes on inside them. That's how we are going to make the greatest strides forward, by harnessing the resources of those people." The employees also got another message, by the way: this organization really cares about me.

Prosperity-conscious people and companies recognize that in difficult times there is danger, but there is also opportunity. Being positive is not pretending there's no risk during difficult times, it is acknowledging the danger while choosing to focus on the opportunity. There are several skills that can assist us in making the choice between prosperity consciousness and poverty consciousness.

We need what I like to call psychological hygiene. Many of us are unaware of the dramatic, sometimes devastating impact that, for example, listening to the news or dealing with certain people has on our inner world. Let's say that I start my day looking through a crystal-clear glass of water. As I'm driving to work I hear on the news that a disaster has occurred somewhere in the world, and that really bothers me. It's like a drop of ink in my glass of water. It spreads through the water, and my world is slightly grayer. Then the sports news comes on and I hear that the Red Sox have blown it again. That's like another drop of ink in the water. Someone cuts in front of me on the expressway. I put the brakes on and get angry—another drop of ink. Pretty soon I'm looking through a gray haze. The world doesn't appear as sharp and as clear as it did first thing in the morning. What has changed? My perception has changed. The thoughts, feelings, and images that I experience color how I view the world in dramatic ways.

If you went through a dangerously contagious hospital ward, you would, immediately upon leaving, engage in hygiene practices. What about psychological hygiene? What about that dreaded disease optical rectumitis? When contaminating influences come into your world, do you take time to wash up, to bring your perception back to where you want it to be by engaging in good mental hygiene practices that allow you to move forward?

Sit down sometime and watch the news. Before it starts, rate yourself from one to ten on how positive you feel. Ten: "I've never felt better in my life." One: "When I die, it will be just a formality." When the news is over, rate yourself again. If you're like most people, you'll feel a little less positive. That's understandable, given the state of the world. But if you become that feeling—if you "awfulize"— you will be paralyzed into inactivity. Worry is not going to help anything you saw on the news. Action will. If we care about dealing with the difficulties that we and others face, we must engage in some psychological hygiene so that we can face the world positively and turn events around. Mother Teresa, as we have noted, wasn't paralyzed by awfulizing. Prosperity-conscious people recognize that at difficult times there is danger, but there is also opportunity.

Reframing

Reframing is a cognitive skill that we can use to consciously identify the opportunities in apparently negative situations. It allows us to move forward, to take a stand and find the energy for what we need in crises. Many large organizations have reframed failures into tremendous opportunities. 3M for example, took a bad batch of glue and turned it into a multimillion-dollar product called Post-it Notes. Some years ago several people died from taking Tylenol that had been tampered with. For many companies, that might have been the disaster that sent them down the tubes. But the way that J&J dealt with the situation—by developing safer containers and telling the public honestly and forthrightly, "There's nothing wrong with our product, but we will temporarily remove it from the shelves and develop a way of sealing containers to ensure public safety," allowed Tylenol to move from disaster to number one in the marketplace. Management capitalized on the events because of the way they viewed the situation and how they chose to deal with it.

Life gives us all kinds of information—"We're only getting a 3% raise," "I'm having trouble with one of my co-workers," "My eldest child has been home late two evenings in a row," "I have to give a speech next weekend and I'm really concerned about it"—but we choose how to view that information. We choose the style of the frame we bring to any situation.

My sister and her husband own a framing shop in West Vancouver, British Columbia. I was visiting the shop with my four children, and Jill and Barry allowed them each to frame a picture that they had purchased on their travels. I was struck by how different frames and different mats changed the look of every picture. Jill would suggest a brown mat for a picture in which I saw no brown, but as soon as the brown mat was put around the picture, all the brown became evident. That's what reframing is about. When you apply different frames—and, if you will, mats—to situations, all sorts of things become apparent, things that were always there but that you could not see before. And each frame will bring out something different in that picture.

In my workshops I often present groups with tough situations and ask them to come up with 10 positive reframings for each situation. Here's one that I use frequently. A junior in a pharmaceutical company was traveling to Stockholm some 15 years ago to make a major presentation to a large international conference. He had uncovered a way of moving products from conception to the marketplace much more quickly than was the norm. The CEO of his organization was traveling with him. On Sunday evening they landed in Stockholm, but their luggage had been placed on the wrong flight and was two-thirds of the way to New Zealand. The presenter was dressed in blue jeans and a golf shirt. All his notes and visual aids were in his suitcase, and he was supposed to be on deck at nine o'clock the next morning. I then ask the workshop participants to give me at least 10 opportunities for him in that situation.

You might take a moment now and see if you can jot down 10 or 12 opportunities. They fall roughly into three categories. First, the "could have been worse" category, which, if you've ever been involved in an automobile accident and are now sitting and reading this book, you know is a legitimate reframing. Second, "lessons for the future." What's that old proverb? "Fool me once, shame on you. Fool me twice, shame on me." And third, "What do I do now?" What are the options open to me right now?

Well, the gentleman in Stockholm decided before he went to bed to write down all the pros and cons of the situation. When he finished, he realized he was in a no-lose position. He saw he had a tremendous opportunity to impress his CEO and to change his presentation style to a more informal one. The following morning he got up and went to the conference center clad in his blue jeans. There the local organizing committee helped him prepare a few overheads for his sales presentation. They were done in Swedish and English, whereas his old overheads had been in English only. He said he'd never had a better storyline and that the audience was instantly sympathetic, as they felt for him because of what he had gone through. Obviously, the incident had not harmed his career—he was a vice president of the pharmaceutical company that had hired me to speak. He considered that incident to be the turning point of his career. It wasn't just because of the nature of his misfortune—it was how he dealt with it that made the difference. He also told me, by the way, that he didn't buy a drink all week. People would say, "There's the guy who lost his luggage. Come on, we'll buy you a beer."

There are tremendous opportunities when we look below the surface of some negative situations. Are the opportunities better than if the situation had never occurred at all? Of course not. Often we do not recoup what we would have had if this person hadn't come into the picture or that incident hadn't happened. But he *has* come into the picture; this *has* happened.

In one case, a client told me about her hidden opportunity. She was a secretary for IBM and had been given the awesome responsibility of bringing coffee to the CEO of the organization when he was touring the local facility. On her way to handing him the coffee, she tripped on the rug and spilled it all over him. He stood there quite shocked, while his juniors patted him dry. At that point the woman broke into uncontrollable laughter at the sight of this man, coffee dripping all over him. Fortunately he joined in the laughter, and they introduced themselves. At the Christmas party that year, when he walked into the room and saw her among the 1,500 people present, he took a wide berth around her and said, "Just stay over there, Mabel. I've got a new suit on." They both laughed. She said, "The important thing about the whole incident, in retrospect, was that I was noticed, and the honest way I responded was appreciated. It turned out that when the CEO was looking for an administrative assistant, I applied for the position and got it. I've since moved up steadily in the organization. This was a turning point in my career."

A parole officer presented the following situation. At her cousin's wedding, her uncle (the father of the bride), being of the old school, had more than $10,000 in an envelope in his tuxedo coat pocket to pay for the hall, food, and drinks following the evening's festivities. He removed his jacket to join in the dancing and hung it on the back of his chair. As the evening wore down, he returned to his chair and discovered the envelope containing the money was missing. Two weeks later, the newlyweds and both sets of parents were watching the wedding video, when clearly, in the background, the father of the groom was seen slipping the envelope containing the money into his own pocket.

It took the workshop participants a few minutes to get over the shock of the woman's story, but they came up with many ingenious reframings, some of which the woman suggested would be helpful for the family. The major thrust of the "opportunities" centered on ensuring that this family problem was dealt with in a way that minimized damage to future relationships. Doing so involved seeing the theft as a cry for help, as if the father-in-law had a serious illness. Of course, the group couldn't resist some humorous offerings, such as "You'll never have to have them all over for dinner."

The next time you're faced with a difficult situation, see if you can sit down and come up with 10 hidden opportunities. Broaden your perspective. Recognize that whether the doorknob is green or blue really isn't significant, it's how you view it. Athletes use this skill all the time. Figure-skating champion Kurt Browning was asked by reporters following his third world championship, "Kurt, how come when you skated second in the short program, you said that was the best place to skate from? When you skate second you don't have long to wait and you can skate well and put a lot of pressure on the athletes who follow you. Yet when you skated near the end, fifth in a group of six in the long program, you said that was the best place to be, because you could see what the others had done and rise above that standard. What's really best, skating second or fifth?" He turned to the reporters and said, "Whatever position you draw out of the hat, you immediately find all of the opportunities in it. There are tremendous opportunities skating first in your group, and last in your group, and in every other position. You just have to look for them". As Kurt Browning has done, it is wise to choose to look for the opportunity in what we're faced with. An old friend once told me that if you were given a barn full of manure to shovel out, it was a tremendous idea to keep in mind that a pony had to be in there somewhere. "Spend your time looking for the pony," he said. "There's no margin in the other stuff."

Self-talk

The concept of self-talk is quite simple: you cannot be the heckler in the crowd at your own performance and hope to be successful. Now, I don't expect that most of you engage in constant negative self-talk—you wouldn't be where you are today if that were true—but remember our concept of trim-tab adjustments. If we can make a small adjustment in self-talk, reframe a little more frequently, perhaps use imagery (which we'll discuss in chapter eight) a little differently—if we can, make a small trim-tab adjustment in these two or three areas, it well make a huge difference down the road.

Imagine, if you will, that you spoke to other people the way you sometimes speak to yourself. One of the athletes I was working with at a recent Olympic Games kept a diary. When I read through a section of it, I found that absolutely everything was expressed in the negative: "Don't do this," and "Don't do that," and "Don't forget this." When I pointed this out, and, more particularly, mentioned that this athlete would never speak to anybody else that way, she remarked, "Isn't that interesting? I constantly emphasize the positive when speaking to others, because I know it's much more productive. I create fewer hassles and I move more quickly to solutions. Yet here I am telling myself what not to do."

Negative messages create what we don't want. If I'm walking into a meeting and I say to myself, "You know nothing's going to come of this. They're never going to buy from me," probably all of my worst expectations will come true. As a friend of mine, Bob Proctor, says, "Millions of people get things every day they don't want, but they expect." But what if I stopped at that instant and said, "Is that what I want?" No, that's not what I want. I want them to buy from me. Then why am I speaking to myself like that? Am I afraid that if I go in expecting something and I don't get it, I will be disappointed? So what? I can handle disappointment. I'll get the disappointment anyway if they don't buy. But why expect it? It's as if we need to prepare ourselves ahead of time for disappointment. Expecting disappointment, however, can affect the outcome in a negative way. Our expectations have a dramatic impact on what we create in our life.

When we communicate with others ideally, we tell them directly what we want. I'm constantly upbraiding coaches about this. It's not "Don't break the pattern too early"; it's "Stay with the pattern and make a proper cut to the ball." Likewise, as parents, it's not "Don't mess up your room"; it's "Make sure your room stays tidy and your books are put back on the shelves when you've finished with them." Tell people what you want, not what you don't want.

In the same way, our self-talk takes a stand for what we want, not what we don't want. People do not wake up in their mid-thirties saying, "Thank goodness, confidence came in the night. I've been waiting for years for confidence to arrive. Now I can get on with my career. Now I can make cold calls. Now I can be the kind of person I've always wanted to be." People acquire confidence by choosing to program themselves for it, by taking a stand for what they want, by talking "as if" they have confidence, even though they don't have it yet. Speed skater Gaetan Boucher, double gold-medal winner in Sarajevo, says, "I had the physical skills to be world champion two or three years before I became world champion. It took me two to three years to learn to think and act like a champion."

We can support ourselves by choosing what we put into the world's finest computer, the human brain. Like a computer, the brain needs a program. A computer cannot take a negative, questionable, doubtful program and produce positive, pro-active, forward results. Computers don't work like that, and neither does the human brain. The brain cannot create things like confidence, or assertiveness, or patience, or integrity out of thin air. We acquire these qualities by programming ourselves for them. Sociologist Louis Wirth said in the preface to Karl Mannheim's *Ideology and Utopia,* "The most important thing that we can know about a man is what he takes for granted." (Wirth was obviously a chauvinist!) What are the underlying, unverbalized assumptions that we operate on everyday and that we never stop to question?

I asked a group of managers in a law office, "What are your inner dialogues with yourself every day?" They came up with the following: "If you're going to get it done right, do it yourself"; "You have to work from dusk-to-dawn to succeed in this job"; "There's not enough time to get everything done that I want to get done"; "I've got to be perfect. If I'm not perfect, people won't appreciate me, and I won't move forward in this organization. I can't make any mistakes." Such assumptions, usually unconscious, if accepted as true, lead to a limited perspective and a high-pressure inner world. Though unconscious, they surface when you pay attention to your inner dialogue. It is important to become aware of this kind of high-pressure self-talk, because it creates inherent tension and therefore undermines health and eventually performance.

I asked the same managers, "Is this an inner climate that allows you to move with calm and certainty through your day? One that allows you to act on things with thoughtfulness, and at a pace that lets you get out all you're capable of doing?" No, of course not. And they were quick to notice that. I asked them to come up with ways in which they could reinforce how they wanted to be and introduced them to the concept of affirmations.

Affirmations

Affirmations are positive statements that take a stand for what you want. They are carefully written, preset sentences that clearly describe the behavior, feeling, and accomplishment that you are seeking. They are, in a way, a form of preprogrammed self-talk. "I walk to the stage confidently and deliver my speech with enthusiasm" would be an affirmation, for example.

In his book *What to Say When You Talk to Yourself,* Dr. Shad Helmstetter gives some vivid examples on how to turn negative self-talk into positive affirmations. "Things aren't going very well for me at work," for example, can be changed to "I enjoy my work. I understand the problems and I get past them." "I wish I had more time" can be changed to "I make time and I take time to do what I need to do" or "I'm responsible for choosing when and where and how I spend my time." These are just a few examples of how negative self-talk can be rewritten to create an inner climate that reflects what you want.

Here are some guidelines for writing affirmations:

1. State your desired behavior simply and in the present tense.
2. Develop two to three statements which reflect what you are working on at any one time.
3. The feelings they elicit are important. Make sure affirm-tions have some punch.
4. Say them to yourself frequently and act as if you are what you say you are.
5. Imagine them occurring.

Because the feelings affirmations elicit are very impor-tant, people have to write their own, or use quotations that grab them. At the turn of the century, Émile Coué, the French psychotherapist, said, "Every day, in every way, I'm getting better and better." And that, for some people, became a powerful affirmation. For others it was a wimpy statement they could never feel comfortable repeating to themselves.

Affirmations are like that. They are individual. Sport, of course, is rife with affirmations. Consider Vince Lombardi's "Winning isn't everything. It's the only thing." Or Muhammad Ali's "Float like a butterfly, sting like a bee." Some people will read a quote that just stops them in their tracks. Others read the same quote and get nothing from it. Many times we run into quotations that really speak to us, but unfortunately we don't capture them, we don't write them down. As a Chinese philosopher once said, "The faintest ink is better than the strongest memory." When you find something that strikes you, don't throw it away. Increase the vocabulary that will move you to where you need or want to be.

I did a workshop for an NHL hockey team. Attending that workshop was George Armstrong, a member of the Hall of Fame and captain of the Toronto Maple Leafs during their heyday. During a break, after I had finished the section on affirmations, George came up to me and said, "You know, I've never talked about this to anybody, but I used to do that all the time. I never called them affirmations, never put it that way. But," he said, "I used to cut quotations and statements out of *Reader's Digest* and the like and put them on file cards, which I kept in my glove compartment. When I was driving to a game, sometimes I'd pull over and go through the box, and I'd find one or two that really hit me that day. That gave me the punch, the power I needed." Well, what George was talking about is a perfect example of affirmations and how to use them.

Perhaps it's best to explain the power of affirmations by telling you some stories about people I have encountered who use them. I recently visited a woman for whom I have tremendous admiration. She has risen to a level in the private sector that is all too uncommon, unfortunately, for women in our society. She had, on the end of her beautiful oak desk, a cardboard tent card upon which she had written, in felt pen, what I would call an affirmation. When I asked her about it, she said, "Oh, my quotation. Well, let me tell you a story first. My father died about four months ago, and I was very close to him. We worked very hard together. He was a role model for me and encouraged me to become what I am today. At the funeral I was very fatigued, having spent two or three days in a funeral home, and I was in that state where often you get a thought, or song, or statement in your head that repeats itself over and over again. The one that I was dwelling on was 'The future is now.' For the first time in my life, I understood what it meant. It doesn't mean that I don't raise my children properly. It doesn't mean I don't buy life insurance, and it doesn't mean that I don't plan for the future. It means I live today. That if I go through my pockets I don't have a ticket that says 'tomorrow.'"

The affirmation on her desk was: It's time to enjoy the thrill of it. I asked, "What does it mean to you when you read that? How do you feel?" She said, "My children will never again be the age they are now. I won't have the same experiences in the years to come that I'm having right now. And even though life is hectic at times, it's time to enjoy the thrill of it." She had written "thrill" in a starburst of colors. She added, "I noticed that I was going through my week like this: 'Oh, no, it's Monday. Head down, body braced, march through the week, eyes on the goal, never look up.' Then at the end of the week, I'd say, 'Hey, it's Friday. I can look around now.' Well, I've realized that Monday, Tuesday, Wednesday, Thursday, and Friday are all days of my life. I choose to do what I am doing. I am not chained to this desk. It's time to enjoy the thrill of it." So she used her affirmation to truly be what I would call a "now-ist," to experience all of what she was going through every day, to be mindful of the experience and to enjoy it as it was happening.

A successful businessman said that his mother always told him, "Never be afraid of falling on your face. It means you were going forward." That affirmation, although he didn't call it an affirmation, allowed him to take risks. A soft-spoken corporate executive once told me that in his early days he was timid and couldn't present his ideas strongly enough in the board room. Many times the discussion would come back to what he had said in the first place, but by then it would appear to have been somebody else's idea. Before entering meetings, he began the practise of repeating an affirmation to himself to ensure that he would be assertive: "No battle was ever won by surrendering." During meetings, he would repeat that to himself in a powerful and emotive way to find the energy and drive to stand up and make his point forcefully and to stick to his guns when he was attacked. "It didn't mean I never backed down," he told me, "but it sure meant that I got my point across and that it got some good argument before it was shot down. The key decision makers began to realize that I had good ideas and they heard the strength with which I was committed to them. It was instrumental in my rise up the organizational ladder."

I met a woman who moved from Lebanon to North

America with her two children because of the uncertain situation in her native country. Her husband had been missing for years, kidnapped by an unknown group. She had a deep sadness about her, but she had an attitude full of positivism that was inspiring. She went to her purse and pulled out a card that she has since plasticized. Written in Arabic, which she translated for me, it said, "There is not enough darkness in the whole world to extinguish the light from one small candle." What a powerful affirmation! Even in the darkest of times, she chooses to move to the light.

There are many other ways to create a "positive" thinking and feeling state within yourself. Reframing, self-talk, and affirmations are cognitive techniques; that is, we consciously choose what thoughts we will focus on for specific situations or changes with which we are dealing. In future chapters, we will explore other perceptual methods as well as physical and imaging techniques for creating positivism.

It is important to note here, however, that controlling and directing the way we choose to view the world, from a positive and personally empowering perspective, is considered by many, including me, a prerequisite for high performance. You may come by this relatively naturally because of your upbringing and personality, or you may be someone who has to work hard to develop it; nevertheless, a positive worldview is essential to the highest levels of performance and health.

CHAPTER FOUR

Active Awareness

You cannot transcend what you do not know. To go beyond yourself, you must know yourself.

—Sri Nisargadatta Maharaj

Someone once remarked, "I'm not sure who discovered water, but you can be certain it wasn't a fish." Active awareness requires us to notice what is happening immediately inside us and around us. Buddha was right—most of us go through life asleep. We are unaware of our inner dimension—the way we tend to think, the images we run, all the nuances of our being that are a product of our past and our current experiences.

Much of the information in this chapter is based on the work of Italian psychiatrist Roberto Assagioli, a colleague of Freud and Jung, who attempted to integrate Eastern philosophy into Western psychology. The concept of disidentification and the material we will be covering on mind, body, and feelings all stem from his work, and I want to acknowledge my debt to him here.

Be patient with this section. It's a little esoteric, but in reality this is an experiential chapter. You will soon have a feeling for what I am saying. You will hear the message, and the concepts will become clear to you.

The foundation for all our inner skills is to be found in the following model:

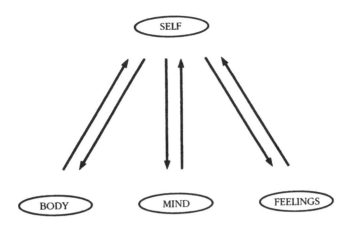

You are not your body. You are not your mind. You are not your feelings. (You have no idea how thrilled I was to discover I was not my body!) I can observe what is going on in my body at any given moment, in any part calling for my attention. I get messages from my body all the time about how rested I am, how strong, or how healthy. I can observe my body, but that is not who I am. I might perceive my heart rate, become aware of tension in my shoulders, notice my breathing, sense that I'm developing a slight headache. I can observe my body, but I am distinct from my body.

I can also observe my feelings. I can go inside myself and notice that I am angry or relaxed, or that I feel safe or unsafe. Some feelings may be subtle. I might not even be able to label them, but I can become aware of the sensations that I call feelings. They can change radically, often from moment to moment, which means I'm certainly not my feelings, because who "I" am doesn't change radically from one moment to the next. I can observe them, I can get information from them, but I am distinct from my feelings.

I can also observe my mind. I might "see" my thoughts, I might hear them speaking to me, but I am distinct from my mind. This is sometimes difficult to accept for those of us who have attended school for a long time. Sometimes when I tell my mind to do something, for example, to stop worrying about what I have to do tomorrow, it doesn't listen to me. So "I" must be separate from my thoughts.

In a workshop I conducted with the coaches for the Canadian Winter Olympic team, one of them said, "I have no trouble with the body and the feeling stuff, but I really believe I am my mind. I can't see separating the two." The next morning when he returned to the workshop, he stopped a group of coaches before we got started. "I have to admit that I now agree with what Peter said yesterday," he began. "Last night, after we all went out and had a few beers and I got back to my room, my body was extremely wrecked. It definitely wanted to go to sleep. I felt very tired. At the feeling state, there is no question that I wanted to go to sleep. Do you think that I could get my mind to shut up so I could nod off?" I said to him. "You got it! You are not your body, you are not your feelings, you are not your mind." That is why you can observe all three.

Who am "I", then? "I" is the part of me that has the capacity to observe all of what is going on in and around me without becoming caught up in it. Each of us can move to a place within ourselves where we can observe what is happening at the mind/body/feeling level and remain unshaken by it. This position of observing, but not being dominated by our inner state, frees us to take the action we choose to take. Otherwise our anger, for example, might determine how we act, rather than our choosing how we want to respond. You can free yourself from being dominated by thoughts and feelings by observing where you are at any one moment. The act of noticing what is happening inside you as you react to the outside world Assagioli called disidentification. The key to disidentification is that you recognize that *what is happening at the mind, body, and feeling levels is what is happening to you, it is not who you are.* You are much more than the sum of these parts. The goal, then, is to move to a place where you can observe, then choose, how you will act. When you move to a position where you are observing, you move to a position where you can control how you will react or behave.

All of who we are doesn't change from moment to moment. Sometimes when we are focused on only one aspect of ourselves we tend to forget about the rest of our being. Imagine for a moment that you are 15 minutes away from making a long, important presentation to your peers. You have been nervous about this for some time, almost afraid. Making presentations is something with which you are familiar; you are good at them. Normally you are little nervous—excited, really—but for some reason that you don't understand, this occasion really has you spooked. The tension has been so great that you have developed a severe cold during the week. So not only are you nervous, you don't feel well, either. You have 15 minutes to go and things are speeding up inside. You are beginning to doubt that you can speak strongly and coherently. Images of blowing it are beginning to surface. What can you do?

Well, first, find a quiet place where you can be alone with your thoughts for a few minutes. Washrooms are good for this. Ask yourself some important questions, starting with "What am I feeling right now?" Observe those feelings, put them out in front of you where you can look at them: "I'm scared, vulnerable, and sick." Listen to your feelings; they will begin to fade once you acknowledge them. The next question is just as helpful. "What else am I?" It is at these times that we need to consciously remind ourselves about all of who we are: "I'm a good presenter, I know my stuff, I'm a very strong person, I'm competent." Right. All of this is true. You may be scared, vulnerable, and sick, but you are also strong, competent, and knowledgeable. These attributes don't go away just because you're scared. You just forget about them. Your strengths get pushed out of your consciousness by your feelings, thoughts, and physiology, and you have to go in, get them, and bring them forward. Developing the ability to hold both positive and negative truths about yourself is empowering. Otherwise, your fear and sickness—not you—will determine how you perform.

I have stood next to several people prior to their winning a world championship. Not one of them said, "Gee, what a beautiful day. I think I'll just go out and win the world title." Every one of them was nervous and upset and anxious, but each one never forgot that he or she had good skills, a tremendous strategy, and a solid program. Now, at life's crucial moments, whether before a world performance, or a job evaluation, or an emotion-charged talk with a friend, it would be nice to diminish the load, to reduce what is going on at the feeling state and inside the mind and body. The three steps involved in active awareness allow you to do just that.

Disidentify, choose, act

The skills that allow us to manage what is going on inside us empower us to change what is going on outside. If we were to divide this strategy into three steps, we would say that
1. we disidentify from our thoughts, feelings, and body—we step back and observe what's going on inside; 2. we activate our will—we choose what we need to balance ourselves; 3. we act—we apply a skill, be it a breathing technique, an image, a positive affirmation, or a reframing that will support the choice we've made.

Consider this situation: I walk into a meeting prepared to make a budget presentation. I have spent a great deal of time preparing, yet about a minute into this important presentation, someone asks a negative and critical question that implies I'm wasting his or her time. If I don't notice that this is making me angry and defensive, then my whole body language changes to defensiveness. My physical stance and my tone of voice change. I pay attention only to the instigator. Throughout the rest of the meeting I make sure only that he or she is hearing what I'm saying. When I leave the meeting I think, when he said that, why didn't I say this or, I forgot to tell her this and this. What happened? I *became* what was happening to me on the inside as a result of that difficult, critical question.

The first step in active awareness—to disidentify—takes only a brief second in many day-to-day situations. Although there are difficult situations for which we might need more time, for the most part we can become proficient at handling daily challenges. We can notice our reaction and shift quite quickly with conscious practice. We notice what is going on and then make a choice. Is it appropriate for me to express my anger and distress here? If I decide that it is, then I do so knowing I've chosen to express my feelings, and I will do so much more effectively. But if I decide that it isn't appropriate, for whatever reason, to express my anger, then I act—I do something. I run an image. I repeat some positive self-talk. I use an affirmation. I use the active-listening skills I learned in the communication course I took last year (we'll be discussing all of these in more detail in the chapters that follow). I choose one of the many clubs I have in my golf bag of coping techniques and I use it to shift from anger to calm. I use skills to change my inner state to improve my outer performance. And by developing numerous skills that I can use in these instances, I can turn distractions such as tough questions into opportunities to get more on my game.

Physical movement

Many people have developed some interesting ways to disidentify. I know a rowing coach who, when he gets upset with what is happening to him, does what he calls a "90-degree jump." He physically jumps 90 degrees to one side. Then he looks back to the spot he's just left and he talks to himself like this: "Well, Bennett, you're really getting in a pickle over that, aren't you? Is it worth it? Come on now, what's really important here? What's important here is that you do this and this." He has physically and emotionally moved to a position where he is in charge again, as opposed to letting his anger and his racing mind take charge.

Imagery

Sometimes metaphors help us learn to disidentify. Images are wonderful for this. I worked recently with a group of people who counsel abused women and children. These counselors have to deal with trauma all day. And so, when the woman who comes in at 9 o'clock leaves at 10 o'clock, it's essential to make sure that all of the emotions and feelings that were discussed in the room leave with her. Any residue will make the counselors less effective with the 10 o'clock arrival. If they hang on to a little of what occurred with her, they will be less effective with the 11 o'clock client, and so on.

In an imagery session, they decided to try an interesting way to disidentify, using the following: "When a client comes in, we imagine she is carrying a ball with her—let's say a red ball—which represents her life. We open the ball up and we do all kinds of things to it that pertain to the experiences in it. We adjust, work on, and practise some of the skills we need to manage what is in that ball. But our final act, as we see the client leaving the office, is to turn and quietly imagine handing the red ball back to her for two good reasons. First, it is her ball; it is her life, and she is the one who has to manage it. And two, doing so helps the quality of our performance by allowing us to disidentify. When we hand her back that ball, we hand her back all of what we have discussed, because the person who is coming through the doorway to replace her is carrying a yellow ball." These counselors can't afford to allow themselves to be overwhelmed by the difficulties they are dealing with. By using the ball image to disidentify, they move to a position where they can truly assist the people who rely on them.

Distractions

By being aware, elite athletes turn apparent distractions into reminders to focus, concentrate, and stick to their strategies. Likewise, in a difficult budget presentation, a tough question is a reminder to get back on your game—to ask for a repeat of the question in order to buy some time to calm yourself down, to make eye contact with all the other members of the committee, and to proceed with the strategy you intended to carry out. It's not a stimulus to be blown off course by the first obstacle you encounter.

Reframing

We can also take control of such situations by choosing to see the question not as a challenge, but simply as a request for information. For years I felt threatened by certain questions that were asked in what seemed like a challenging or skeptical tone from someone in the audience. I acted defensively and aggressively in response. When I reframed these questions as requests for information, I was able to reduce the impact they had on me. I say to myself when I feel that initial fear: "This person doesn't understand. This person wants more information. Listen to the question." By choosing to perceive all questions simply as requests for information, I move to the fair witness position, a place where I can truly hear the question and access all of the information I need to respond in a manner and tone that are caring and concerned.

Communication with self and others

Perhaps you've recognized by now that the mind, the body, and the feelings are two-way channels of communication. We not only receive information, but we transmit messages at all three levels. Let's look first at outside communication. We are all aware that the body language and images we receive from other people communicate a good portion of the messages that we pick up from them. It's not only what we hear at the mind level that gives us their message, but also what we receive at the body level and at the feeling level.

The most difficult messages that we receive from other people are incongruent messages, those that say one thing, for example, at the mind level and another at the body level. For instance, someone may tell you she loves you, but when she puts an arm around you, it feels like three yards of cement. The mind message says, "I love you"; the body message says, "Not a chance." Or someone tells you in a defensive, hostile tone, "I'm not upset with what you said. I just don't want to talk about it." At the mind level the message is "Everything's fine"; at the feeling level it's "You turkey." Those messages are difficult to deal with. When we communicate with other people and ourselves, it's critical that we convey the same message at all three levels.

I recently attended a figure-skating practice with Doug Leigh, coach to Brian Orser, Elvis Stojko, and many other fine, world-class figure skaters. We were working with a young woman who had recently lost quite a lot of weight and thus had changed her body type to a fair degree. It was, of course, affecting her skating. I asked Doug how she was doing. "Awful," he said, "she's skating brutally. She can't land her jumps. Her balance is off." The young woman skated over. She looked dejected, as if she were expecting Doug to just give up on her. "I'm skating like shit," she said. "Yes, you are. But do you see these two feet?" he said, pointing to his own feet. "They aren't going anywhere. They're staying right here. You are working hard. You are doing everything right. You just have to stick with it until you get used to how it feels. I'm here with you and I'm going nowhere, because I know that we can get this."

Doug gave a congruent message that left no room for interpretation on her part. If he had been less direct, afraid to acknowledge the reality, or if he had left any room into which her own doubt could wiggle, the message would have been less effective. Instead that skater receives a powerful message: "I believe in you and I'm with you." Doug said it with feeling; he said it with his mind; and he said it with his body. He gave her an image to hold on to. Thus she was able to make a transition fairly quickly to the skater she needed to be in to try her jumps again.

Acting "as if"

Well, the same principles apply when we communicate with ourselves. The more levels that we can communicate on, the better. That's why acting "as if" is so critical, because when we act "as if" at the body level, we are transmitting a positive message that can help move us to where we want to be. Do you realize that if you smile for eight to ten seconds, there's a measurable change in your blood chemistry? Roberto Assagioli wrote a fair amount about acting "as if." In many ways, he said, the technique makes use of the same dynamic power as imagery. But in this instance we use actions instead of images to create the internal emotional state that we desire. Probably the simplest example of this is singing or whistling to bolster your courage as you head through a lonely or scary place at night. We do something physical to support our choice to be brave. We communicate with or direct our bodies to act in ways that will help us be and do what we really want.

Many athletes, on awakening the morning of an important competition, will not get out of bed until they create within themselves the inner climate that they need to perform. Many times negative processes have gone on during the night at the subconscious level, and they may not wake up in the best frame of mind. Lying there smiling, replaying some positive dreams and beginning to act the way they want to be, allows them to create the inner state that they need at that moment.

If we also engage in self-talk or affirmations at the mind level, giving ourselves the same message, then we will make a quicker transition to confidence and assurance than if we were operating at just one level. Using multilevel skills, skills that cover the message board at all three levels, helps us to make interior transitions quickly in difficult moments, whether we're dealing with a loved one or about to make a presentation to a group of people.

Many of us have skill sets that really don't match the problems we need to address. I was preparing a videotape and workshop for a group of medical practitioners from across the United States. In order to meet their needs in the workshop, I had asked them three preliminary questions. The first question was, "What are the high-pressure situations in your life?" Their answers varied a great deal, but here are a few examples:

- confrontation; angry patients, negative co-workers
- heavy work loads with multiple deadlines
- operating on attorneys or members of their family

And then I asked them, "What impact do these high-pressure situations have on you? What happens to you as a result?" Some typical responses were anxiety, worry, discomfort, nervousness, tension, uneasiness, feeling out of control, defensiveness, impatience, futility, lack of concentration, and so on. The list could go on and on, as you can imagine.

And then I asked, "What skills do you use to deal with these situations?" and here's what they said:

- Take time and reorganize.
- Prepare better.
- Concentrate harder on the task at hand.
- Organize well; use my time well.
- Keep thinking, I will survive, and fight through it.
- Try to ignore it.

Now, it's clear from these lists that there is an incongruency between the types of skills that these people were employing and the problems they faced. They identified physical, organizational skills in trying to deal with problems that were clearly mental and emotional. It's as if they had no sand wedge in their golf bag, yet they consistently found themselves in the sand trap. To deal with anxiety, worry, discomfort, nervousness, and frustration, they needed some skills to go inside at the feeling, body, and mind level. Most of the skills they identified were things outside themselves, physical actions. And the problems? The problems were inside.

A Sufi was feverishly searching under a street lamp when his master approached. "What are you looking for?" asked the master. "My keys," replied the Sufi. "Where did you lose them?" his master asked. "Over there," said the Sufi, pointing to the darkness beyond the light. "Then why are you looking over here?" asked the master. "Because," replied the Sufi, "the light is so much better here."

Like the Sufi, we often look for the "key" only in well-lit, familiar places. We often try to apply skills that have worked for us in the past—organizational skills, trying-harder skills—but we attribute what has gone wrong to the inner dimension. Developing skills that allow us to work on the inner dimension is like shining a light into the darkened areas so that we can look for the keys in the place they are most likely to be found.

The importance of action

Centuries ago a Chinese philosopher said, "To know and not act is not to know." Understanding and awareness are not enough in and of themselves. I will be making constant reference throughout this book to acting on our own behalf. Action is a key element in awareness. It moves us from theory to practice, from observation to practical application. There are four levels of awareness in high performance:

1. **Unconscious incompetence:** This is not a level of performance; it's a level of nonperformance. At this level, we don't know any better; we're not aware of how our inner-state is dramatically affecting our performance. It's like not being aware that we shouldn't pickup heavy objects in an awkward manner by reaching over to the side with our back twisted.

2. **Conscious incompetence:** Someone says to me, "Hey, Jensen, don't pick up objects like that—you're going to hurt your back." I say, "Thank you very much," and continue to do it the same way. I insist that I come from a long line of strong backs, or that it's quicker this way. I am "consciously incompetent." I'm aware, but I choose not to act. It's the "yes, but" syndrome, I know I should be more patient; I know I should be dealing with some of

the things that are happening to me; I know I should develop a sense of humor. I know I should lift the chair differently, but I don't. There is a barrier between this level of awareness and high performance. And, of course, the barrier is action—we have to choose to do something.

3. **Conscious competence:** This requires active awareness and attentive practice. When we become consciously competent we choose to do something. We recognize what is happening to us; we become aware and we act on that awareness. When picking up a chair, I remind myself, "Turn all the way around; bend your knees, etc." On noticing that I'm getting angry, I remind myself to apply my inner skills; I calm myself down and I take action on my own behalf.

4. **Unconscious competence:** Automatic expertise. Clearly, the highest level of performance occurs when I automatically apply inner skills and techniques; I automatically pickup chairs quickly and efficiently, using proper body mechanics. We have thousands of things that we do at the unconsciously competent level that we have learned through attentive practise.

Customer service

Let's look at the area of customer service as an external example of the above four steps. If I'm not aware that my product is not well received in the marketplace—that it's breaking down or dripping oil, for instance—then I am at the first level, unconscious incompetence. If, however, several customers phone with complaints, I then move to the second level. Now, if I say, "What the heck's wrong with them? I mean, we make a good product," then I'm never going to move into the realm of excellence. I will always remain at the level of conscious incompetence. At the third level, despite how difficult conscious competence is, I listen carefully to what my customers say and I make modifications and adjustments based on their suggestions. Finally, at the fourth level, unconscious competence, I automatically follow up with my customers. I automatically hear their concerns and, without defensiveness, make modifications and adjustments as they are warranted.

What about the internal customer—*you?* What about servicing *you* with excellence by becoming aware of what is happening to you as a result of what you are facing, and choosing to take some action to satisfy *you,* the internal customer. By choosing to engage in active awareness, we can move to a place where we are in control of what we do through the three simple steps presented in this chapter: disidentify, choose, act.

Separating yourself from your performance

Sometimes in life we become very identified—overidentified—with what we do. (This is an easy and common distortion for athletes.) We begin to believe that all of who we are is connected only to what we do out there in the world. Therefore, if we're not doing well—we're making mistakes, progressing too slowly, failing—we believe that we are a mistake, we are slow, we are a failure. Overidentification with our actions can lead to poor performance and health.

You are not the last meeting you conducted, the last disciplinary action you took with one of your children, the last phone call you made, the last report you wrote. You are much more than those things. I'm not saying don't care about the quality of the report, or the nature of the interaction you had with your child; rather, I'm saying care so much that you do not become what you are doing. When we become what we are doing, we are destined to ride an emotional roller coaster—up to the heights with the highs and down to the depths with the lows.

I was working one day with one of the top female tennis players. She was having a lesson on returning balls hit deep to her backhand, which required her to run back and hit high-bouncing balls cross-court with a top spin, into a target deep on the other court. This is a difficult skill to master. About 20 minutes into the drill, she got into a state that I'm sure you'll all recognize. She started to get in the way of her own performance. She hadn't hit the ball into the target more than three or four times, and despite her coach's patient instruction and feeding her balls, she was beginning to really get down on herself. Eventually, in total frustration she threw her racket to the ground and walked over to her coach. I'll censor her comments: "You must really be upset with me," she said."You're patiently feeding me these tennis balls, and I haven't hit a darned one into the target." The coach looked surprised. "You?" he said. "I'm fine with you. You're working hard, you're pushing yourself, you're trying your best. I just don't like what the tennis ball is doing. I want it to spin like this," he said, indicating top spin with his hands.

What a wonderful teaching moment! He taught her that she is not her backhand; her backhand is that shot she hits over on that side of the court. The minute she becomes her backhand, the minute she wears it as if it were a suit of clothes, what happens to the rest of her game? She undermines her drive or ambition. She doesn't move as quickly on the court. Her volleys aren't as crisp. There's a slight hesitation in her second serve. She undermines everything she needs to get over a bad backhand, and she lowers the entire level of her game. When we constantly judge how things are going as we are doing them or immediately upon finishing them, when we bring down the gavel and say, "No! That was lousy," and what we're really experiencing is "I am lousy," we lose the lesson.

I was working with some discus throwers. One of them, upon the release of the discus, would say, "No, that's not right!" Not only did he throw away the discus, he threw away the lesson, as well. A great amount of what he was doing was right, but in his anguish—in his becoming the bad throw—he lost all the information he needed to make a better one. I jokingly brought him a gavel to the next practice. "Here," I said, "you can bang this down every time you make a judgment or a pronouncement." We talked about separating himself from the throw so that he could take a position where he could see what was going on. In other words, to be upset with that throw, but to be okay with himself.

A football coach was working with a wide receiver on running proper patterns. The receiver was disturbed because he had become the improperly run patterns and the dropped balls. The coach called him over to the sideline and pointed at the field. "I'm very upset about that pattern out there," he said. "You're standing over here. I know you can do that pattern out there. I'm fine with you, but I want that pattern to go down 10 yards, take a sharp 90-degree turn to the middle and break upfield." That not only enabled the athlete to use his imagery skills (which we will discuss later) to see what was taking place, but it also separated the athlete from the pattern; it allowed him to see it, and be free to try it.

As coaches—and all of us are coaches, as parents, with co-workers, and so on—we need to help others separate themselves from their performances. Suppose I'm an uncertain, unconfident junior executive who brings a report that is merely background information to you and your committee. If no one takes the time to separate me from the report, if no one says, "Great background work, Jensen, but we're going to tear this to shreds and you won't even recognize it in five minutes," when the report gets reorganized and rearranged, I might as well crawl on the table as well, because it will feel as if I'm being torn apart. But if someone takes a minute to say, "Great report, Jensen. We appreciate your effort and the background information. We are going to reorganize this totally, but you've saved us 10 hours of work," it makes all the difference in the world.

At a meeting of Performance Coaching Inc., we took ordinary beanbags with the word *idea* written on them and distributed them to each of the members sitting around the conference-room table. Whenever any of us had an idea, we'd say, "Well, here's an idea," and we'd throw our beanbag into the middle of the table. We imagined that the idea was the beanbag. When we were being critical of the idea, we weren't being critical of others sitting around the table, just the idea that was truly out on the table. Now, this may sound silly to you, but it allowed us to separate ourselves, to let go of our ideas, and to move more quickly through the meeting. We didn't have to protect anyone by prefacing our remarks so as not to upset the person whose idea was on the table. With my children I take the approach "You I love, but I very much dislike your behavior toward your younger sister." Separating the person from the action and separating ourselves from what we are doing allows us to learn life's lessons.

Eleanor Roosevelt, the outspoken First Lady, was a master at separating herself from what was being said about her. In one instance, when a group of people asked her how she could possibly stand all the criticism that was being leveled at her by various members of the media for her outspokenness, she turned to the questioner and said, "My dear, they're not criticizing me. They're criticizing the First Lady." She definitely understood how to separate herself from her performance.

In summary, the most important skill to develop in the area of active awareness is the ability to disidentify (step back and observe) from disruptive thoughts, feelings, and images, and to identify (choose) thoughts, images and actions that will strengthen and empower us to perform in ways that are aligned with our goals. In doing this, it is important to remember that we can hold two apparently opposing truths, for example: "I am tired" and "I am strong." Remember the three steps: 1. Disidentify—observe; 2. Choose—identify with your will; 3. Act—do something to support your choice.

We can find many ways to cue and assist ourselves in using our awareness in an active way: for example, feelings, metaphors, distractions, and physical movement. It is also helpful to remember that when we communicate with others, the more congruent our message is at all three levels, the more effective the message will be. Words, body language, and the pictures we paint enhance or confuse the message.

Finally, it is important to recognize that in dealing with feelings such as anxiety, fear, or anger, using organizational and time-management skills alone is not enough to elevate ourselves to the highest performance levels. You don't rehabilitate the knee if the back is damaged. Use the skills outlined in the rest of this book to communicate with yourself at the emotional, imaginational, and physical levels. Talk to the part of yourself that needs the attention, and, when under extreme pressure, talk to all of who you are.

CHAPTER FIVE

Energy Management

The world is too much with us.
                              —Wordsworth

When I conducted a workshop for a large and complex social-service agency, the head of the agency stood up to introduce me to his field workers and began his introduction with the following:

The major theme for today, if not for this decade, was introduced 400 years ago by William Shakespeare. In about 1598 he wrote a play called *Hamlet.* Let me give you a brief synopsis, to refresh your memory. Hamlet awoke one morning to find that everything had changed. His whole life had undergone remarkable upheaval. His father was dead; his mother was sleeping with his uncle (well, not exactly sleeping—that's what bothered him so much); his best friend had left the country; his fiancée had jumped into the lake and floated away; and two of his old school chums were trying to kill him. And if that wasn't enough, every night his father's ghost appeared and bade him to do something about this mess.

But Hamlet could do nothing. He was paralyzed by change. He spent the days wandering around asking himself questions that he could not answer, such as "To be, or not to be..." He even spent time talking to dead people. Then he had a revelation. He realized "There is nothing either good or bad, but thinking makes it so." What Hamlet realized was that change itself was just change. It wasn't good or bad, it was just different. And what made "different" good or bad was how he reacted to it. Unfortunately for Hamlet, he didn't heed his own wisdom; he died in Act V.

With caseloads swelling and budget constraints pressing down from above, social workers certainly need to develop good energy-management skills. Otherwise, the nature of the work can lead to burnout and a sense of hopelessness. It is not my intention to discuss all of the numerous external obstacles to sound energy management: a pace of change that would make Hamlet turn in his grave; heavy workloads; balancing multiple roles; increased traffic, to name but a few. These are all givens of Western culture in the new millenium. But let's examine the inner dimension (that is, how we think and feel about these issues and the impact they have on our personal energy level), because ultimately that's where stress occurs, and that's where we can exert the most control over our lives. Situations of and by themselves don't lead to difficulty in energy management. Situations are not stressed; people are.

When asked after his retirement what he missed most about playing professional football, Fran Tarkenton, who was a Hall of Fame quarterback for the Minnesota Vikings before he became the Ed McMahon of the "Anthony Robbins Show," replied, "You know what I miss? I miss walking up behind the center. The crowd is screaming. There's 10 seconds left in the game. We're down by six points. Millions are watching on television, and absolutely everything depends on what I do at that moment. I miss that."

Now, for most of us that would be a high-stress situation, leading to dramatic energy mismanagement and poor performance. For some, however, it's a challenge—something to look forward to. As was the case with positivism (and with Hamlet), so much of energy management has to do with the perception we bring to events. There is no question that the "hurry-up" offense mentality of Western society encourages energy mismanagement and distorted values.

If you're stuck in traffic, do you put your car in neutral and push the gas pedal halfway to the floor? Not likely. You wouldn't waste the energy (gasoline), and you wouldn't want to damage the engine of the car. Yet how many of us stuck in that same traffic jam put our inner gas pedal three-quarters of the way to the floor, thereby wasting our energy and damaging a much more important engine, our body, despite the fact we can go nowhere.

In a wonderful book called *The Age of Unreason,* author Charles Handy presents a grisly metaphor for the way we live our lives. He says that if you take a frog and drop it into boiling water, the frog will jump out and save its life. If, on the other hand, you put a frog into lukewarm water and gradually heat it, eventually the frog will die. What is the temperature of the water you're in today compared with what it was 10 or 20 years ago? And how often do you try to manage your current environment with skills you learned 20 years ago?

The body is a reliable messenger—it faithfully tells us when we are mismanaging our energy. We mismanage our energy for any number of "good" reasons, such as:

- pressure at work and at home
- time compression
- poor time management
- emotional distress because of an argument
- poor performance and feelings of inadequacy
- money problems

Our body lets us know at three levels:

1. **The body level:** Physical symptoms, such as rashes or a sore back, manifest themselves.
2. **The emotional level:** We become mired in negative feelings, pent-up emotions.
3. **The behavioral level:** We lose patience. We speak too quickly.

Each of us has a different oil light. For some, it's a sore back; others miss the meaning of jokes; some feel flat and unmotivated; still others get migraines. These may all be signs that we are doing a poor job of dealing with life and work stress and mismanaging our energy. Now, when the oil light comes on in your car, you wouldn't take masking tape, lay it over the oil light, and say, "Cleaned that sucker up." If you did that, your engine would eventually burn out. Well, surprise, surprise! The same is true of us. When we don't manage our energy properly, eventually our engine gives out.

In an article in the *Journal of the American Medical Association,* it was estimated that stress is a precipitating factor in 80 percent of all illnesses. Many forms of illness are directly related to our ability, or rather inability, to manage our energy properly. If stress were a bacteria or a virus, imagine the millions of research dollars that would be spent trying to deal with this epidemic. Because stress, by and large, has to do with what goes on inside people, it's largely ignored.

Heading for burnout

Sometimes the pressure that leads to increased inner tension and energy mismanagement isn't related to a single event. It may be the result of long-term issues (the relentless personal pressure of a sick child), a constricting worldview (one that holds that if things are going well something bad is going to happen), an unreasonable set of expectations ("I must be perfect"), or a work load that never slackens. Although habits in dealing with these may seem impossible to change, millions of people change them every year—particularly people who develop serious illnesses. These people might have argued vehemently that they could never make a significant change in their lives. Yet two or three days after they discover they have a life-threatening illness, they find ways to make the very change they had insisted was impossible.

I'm sure you've had the experience of being in a room where there was a background noise that you didn't notice until it disappeared. I sometimes think of stress (which I relate directly to energy management) as a fan. The fan starts slowly, and you barely hear the motor humming. But if you're not careful, three or four weeks later the motor is roaring, and you aren't even hearing it. You aren't hearing it because you're out of touch with what is happening to you. And it's only when the fan goes off that you realize it was on.

A woman in my workshop described it well. She said that when her energy level is up for a long period of time, when she is going nonstop for an extended period, she stops noticing what she's doing to her home life. "When I'm high for too long," she said, "I forget to eat. I miss sleep. I don't notice what's happening to me, to my relationships, and to my children." We will see, under Energy Management and Performance, that there is a physiological reason for this. When energy level is high, attentional focus gets narrow and important variables are missed.

Acting as if you have time

The self-talk that we repeat over and over to ourselves and that puts pressure and constraints upon us—or, in other words, our general assumptions about life—leads directly to energy mismanagement. One subject we frequently develop distorted assumptions about is time. What types of self-talk do you engage in concerning time?

Dr. Larry Dossey, a Texas physician, wrote a book called *Space, Time and Medicine*. In it, he points out that our concept of time is at the root of many of the illnesses we face. We carry around within us a bias that need not be true: that there is not enough time, that we are under time pressure, that we are constantly under deadline constraints. In reality, we create and reinforce most of this perception ourselves by the way we talk to ourselves.

"If only I had more time...time flies...I had a great time...I had a lousy time...time just ran out on us...it's time to get up...It's time to go to work...it's time to go to bed...I've got to get there on time..." Just read through that list and feel the impact those statements have on you. Our beliefs about time deeply influence our general, everyday, getting through-life arousal level. Likewise, the whole notion of "have to"—we have to have this, and we have to have that—creates a pace and pressure that are totally unrealistic. But our overachieving, time-pressured, North American outlook can be changed and replaced with a belief system that allows us to slow time down.

It is worthwhile to distinguish between chronological time (the clock on the wall) and psychological time (our perception of time). We can dramatically slow down psychological time by choosing to act as if, to move as if, to talk as if we have time. We acquire time by choosing at the mind, body, and feeling levels to act as if there is ample time at our disposal.

What we feel at any one time is an accumulation of all the various places we are focusing our attention. Many times we are being "now-ist," "then-ist," and "when-ist." We are trying to pay attention not only to what we are doing now, but also to things that have already happened and to things that we want to happen. When we become accustomed to this as a mindset, we increase our arousal level and our pace, and we "act as if" we do not have all the time we need to get things done right now.

When, for example, I sit down to review my schedule and look ahead to what I am supposed to do next week, then turn the pages and get involved in the following weeks, and pretty soon the next five or six months, I feel a tremendous sense of urgency and panic. It's as if I have to do all of these things now, when in reality, of course, I am going to do them one meeting at a time, one day at a time, one week at a time, one month at a time, and one year at a time. If I'm not careful, I will put an incredible amount of pressure on myself.

On the other hand, imagine what you can accomplish with the kind of belief system depicted in these affirmations:

- I have all the time I need to do my tasks.
- Live now.
- There is time for all paths.
- Don't postpone joy.

Imagine a quilt, or a mélange, of these affirmations, or any others that capture the multifaceted, well-balanced you that you wish to be.

At the 1988 Calgary Olympics I had the pleasure of working with the ice-dance team of Robert McCall and Tracy Wilson. Although they were probably the finest ice dancers in the world, they went home with the bronze medal (there are no politics like ice-dancing politics—but that's another story). Their program, a high-paced ragtime piece that involved well over 3,000 fast, synchronized movements, covered more ice than any other team's. Sometimes when I'd watch them practice, the music would finish and they'd still continue dancing for another 10 seconds. I'd turn to the coaches and say, "You know, there's just too much material, given their music. They went through that as quickly as they could." And the coaches would look at me knowingly and nod patronizingly. Then I'd watch the same routine during the afternoon practise, and there would actually be pauses between the sections of the dance, and they would get all the movements in easily in the 4 minutes and 12 seconds of music.

What was the difference between the morning practise and the afternoon practise? I soon discovered that it was the mindset they took to the dance. I vividly recall our conversation in Calgary seconds before they went on the ice. We used to talk about the mood of the dance. "What words capture this dance for you?" I'd ask. They'd use phrases like "It's a smoky poolroom"; "It's misty"; "It's sensual." But we had also started to include images about time. I remember Tracy saying, "I've trained for 15 years and I want to stay out there forever." Robert said, "I'm going to make every movement last. I'm going to act as if we had all the time in the world." That was the mindset they took on the ice to do more than 3,000 lightning-quick movements.

If they had said, "Okay, hold on now! We've got 4 minutes and 12 seconds to do 3,212 movements. Let's go. Let's get at it," that mindset would not have allowed them to get out all of their abilities. Paradoxically, if they had rushed, they would not have been able to fit in all of the dance during the allotted time, and that would have had a dramatic negative impact on the quality of their performance. By choosing a mindset that allowed them to slow down and act as if they had time, they chose a mindset that allowed them to be highly successful.

Learning to act as if you have time, learning to be a "now-ist," is not only good for your health, but for your performance. I think, for example, of the marketing manager who was trying to combine two sales staffs and two marketing departments as a result of a merger of two organizations. He had to review more than 100 different positions, interview staff, make decisions on career paths, as well as dismiss a fair number of employees. On the end of his desk he had an affirmation that said, "There is time for all paths." When I asked him about it, he explained that when he got out of joint because of the strain and stress of his job and he was trying to consider one situation while thinking of five others, he looked at that affirmation and reminded himself, "If I move through each situation and give it my full attention, I will get the work done a lot quicker than trying to do bits and pieces of each simultaneously."

Years ago psychologists determined that we can hold seven pieces of information, plus or minus two, at any one time. That's why phone numbers are seven digits long; if they were eight or nine digits we would have a hard time remembering them. Think of the seven bits of information as a film loop in which there is a bit of information in each of its seven frames. If four of the frames are focused on what you are doing now and three are focused on other things, that film loop has to move very quickly in order to maintain a clear picture of the four frames you wish to concentrate on. If, on the other hand, all seven frames contain the same information, you are truly focused on what you are doing; you are truly being a "now-ist." Then the film can move slowly in order to project a clear image of what you are doing.

When discussing their tennis match, hockey game, or the great catch of the football game, elite performers constantly make reference to their perception of time at that moment. They use terms such as "playing in the zone," "in sync," "as if I just went out there." "But," they say, "suddenly the game is over, and yet, when I think back to any point in the game, it's as if everything were appearing in slow motion. I could see so clearly my choices and what I had to do." It's as if the ball or the puck had slowed down. Everything was sharp and clear.

Learning to act as if we have time makes us change our perceptions of time. When you go into your office after-hours and no one is there, it's amazing how much work you get done because you can focus on each task separately. You look up at the clock and three hours have gone by, and you've done the work that would normally take a day or two to do, because you are truly a "now-ist" at that moment. Learning to act as if we have time in high-paced multiple-information environments is crucial, because, like it or not, we can only do one thing at a time.

Studies have shown that when you take subjects and play one radio program to them through one earphone and a second through another, it's clear that their attention shifts from one program to the other and back again. People think they have heard them both in their entirety; they have not. We focus on one thing at a time, and when our mind flips from subject to subject, everything speeds up. Our film loop moves quickly. We appear rushed and harried; our perception becomes rushed and harried; and therefore everything becomes rushed and harried.

In *The Three Minute Mediator*, author David Harp talks about walking as if you have time. Instead of worrying and scurrying from one appointment to the next, walk and breathe so that each step soothes and centers the mind. In his book, *Peace Is Every Step*, Thich Nhat Hanh, the Vietnamese Zen poet and 1967 nominee for the Nobel Peace Prize, reminds us that in the rush of modern life, we tend to lose touch with the peace that is available in each moment. His creativity lies in his ability to make use of everyday signals—a ringing telephone, red lights, or traffic jams—as pathways to mindfulness, where he is truly aware of all the nuances of whatever he is doing at the moment. Peace is not external, he says, but by living mindfully, slowing down and enjoying each breath, you will find your inner peace.

I was at the world Water Ski Championships in 1985 in Toulouse, France, working with a skier named Judy McClintock. On the day that she won the world trick championship, thousands of spectators lined the sides of the long, narrow lake, watching the competition. Judy and I had gone to the end of a lake in a children's playground to relax, because you do not do intricate, high-speed tricks at a high-arousal, high-energy level. You relax and allow the tricks to happen—to flow.

Judy had done a good job of relaxing to the point at which she was in charge of her energy, bringing herself down to an appropriate level, given the task at hand. Then she realized that she would prefer to change the harness on one of her skis, but she had to go back to the dressing room, which was about a quarter of a mile away, to get the other harness. I said to her, "Judy, walk. Walk slowly all the way there and all the way back." She told me afterward that it was the longest walk she had ever taken in her life. Everything in her body screamed to hurry up, to rush, yet she had lots of time. So at the body level and at the feeling level, she reinforced the message that she had time. By acting as if she had time, she acquired plenty of it.

Every once in a while, a story metaphorically captures the true importance of time and the perspective we bring to it. A man was walking by a farm one day. The farmer was patiently lifting pigs up, one by one, to an apple tree where they would chew off an apple. The man said to the farmer, "Why do you do it that way? Doesn't it take a lot of time?" "Yes," the farmer conceded, "but time don't mean nothing to a pig."

Humor

Humor is a wonderful skill in helping us to manage our energy. To elite athletes I have often jokingly said, "The situation is hopeless, but not serious." With that attitude, the strain of the challenge immediately falls away. My business manager, Shelley Swallow, has a wonderful quotation above her desk. It says, "Angels can fly because they take themselves lightly." We would all fly a lot farther, higher, and with greater ease if we took ourselves more lightly. Author Norman Cousins (The Healing Heart) referred to laughter as internal jogging and demonstrated that humor was connected to personal health.

A well-delivered line, a clever joke, can cut through pressure and tension in laserlike fashion. Humor and playfulness are a big part of my approach with coaches and athletes during the tense moments before important performances. At the World Figure Skating Championships in

Cincinnati in 1987, Brian Orser was skating his program during the last practice before the biggest event of his life. An inexperienced Korean skater who was in the practice group of six went into a spin at center ice. The loose change that he inexplicably had in his track jacket windmilled out onto the ice. As the warm coins quickly melted into the ice, he feverishly tried to gather his change on his hands and knees; meanwhile Orser approached in full flight. Brian had to abandon most of his program, and was visibly irritated when he reached his coach, Doug Leigh, and me at the boards. With a deadpan face and a serious tone I said to Brian, "After extensive negotiations with the leading figure-skating authorities, we have been assured that the Korean competitor will not be on the ice when you skate your program tonight." Brian's tension and agitation broke. It so happens he won the world championship that night.

I was standing with one of the world's leading coaches in Munich at a world championship. His athletes were in their final preparation, and there was an air of seriousness as he barked out his commands—coaches can also get to energy levels that aren't ideal for effectively dealing with what is happening around them. A well-dressed women approached and said to me in a loud, accented voice, "We are collecting the autographs of the finest coaches in the world, and we see you with some of the best athletes. You are one of the great coaches; we would like you to sign our book of honor."

"By all means", I replied, as my compatriot stared straight ahead in disbelief. I signed with great aplomb and ceremony.

As she moved away, I called after her, "My assistant here will someday be a great coach. Perhaps you would like his autograph, as well."

"Oh, thank you, yes," she replied, pushing the book forward.

In an unparalleled display of self-control, the coach signed the book. What he said after she moved out of earshot is mostly unprintable, but the tension broke and he got great mileage out of the story over the next few days.

Humor need not be reserved for only those times when others are present. I have had more than a few good laughs at myself in the midst of situations where I was over-energized. At the Albertville Olympics I was rushing from the ice to the dressing room to get something. As I strode out of the change room, having retrieved the object, I tried to turn out the light, but no matter which switch I flicked, the room remained bright. It took a few minutes for me to realize that there was a skylight in the ceiling, and only night could turn it out. I laughed and was thankful for such a clear (and humorous) signal—I was mismanaging my energy. A woman in my workshop told me how she noticed she was under stress and not coping well—she found her car keys in the refrigerator. She had a good laugh and noted the lesson in energy mismanagement.

A lighthearted approach not only reduces the tension, but also helps put the real-life importance of events into perspective. It helps distinguish what is truly serious (life-threatening situations) from the day-to-day hassles of living. Most of what we do in our lives is not serious. When we lose the humor present in everyday affairs, we lose perspective, which dramatically raises our tension level and leads to unsatisfactory performances.

Some offices have started deliberately injecting humor into the work environment to reduce stress and strain. Chicago humorologist Steve Wilson cites the example of the "Oh, no!" squad. When the photocopy machine jams, for example, and someone gets all upset and out of sorts about it, mismanaging energy dramatically (which will affect how the person feels, her confidence, and how she works the rest of the day), the "Oh, no!" squad swings into action, popping on Styrofoam clown noses. They walk over, shake their heads, and exclaim, "Oh, no! Oh, no! Oh, no!" The sight of colleagues with clown noses, shaking their heads, quickly releases the anger and pent-up emotion over the photocopy problem, which allows some perspective. Everybody moves back to work in a better frame of mind.

One of my workshops participants told me a story that happened when he and his wife moved into their new home. Rick likes to argue everything out, and his wife does not like confrontation at all. One day he decided that he had to have it out with her over an issue, but she did not want to be confronted with it. He followed her all around the new house, but she kept walking away from him, until finally she went downstairs into the basement, where there was nothing but a shower surrounded by a lot of packing cartons. He followed her into the shower, determined to have the confrontation. They were standing there both fully clothed, and she turned on the shower to drown Rick out. "That broke the ice," he said. "We both killed ourselves laughing, then we relaxed and were able to work things out."

Some long-term skills

The energy-management skills outlined here, like those discussed under Positivism, are designed to help you lessen the impact of external forces and internal belief systems on your arousal level. In fact, many of the skills we've already discussed—for example, reframing—can help you improve your perception about how you are expending your energy. Reframing is the skill that allows us to find the true opportunities in difficult situations. Likewise, self-talk and practicing affirmations that take a stand for how we want to be can be energy regulators.

I believe that the ability to relax and lower your energy level when you need to is a critical skill. It's almost an essential skill if you work in a high-paced, high-pressure environment. Most of us have no trouble getting pumped up for key events, but we go too high, then have no way of coming down quickly to gain some perspective and manage our energy effectively.

Long-term energy-management techniques combine all of the skill areas we discuss in this book. Dr. Herbert Benson called the set of physiological factors he found in deep relaxation "the relaxation response." He outlined four simple-to-follow steps in order to access this incredible calm. The response is built into every human body; it is innate. Therefore, the ability to relax deeply comes from learning to elicit this innate response. (By the way, this type of relaxation is not akin to soft music and a glass of wine, although those are also excellent for personal health and well-being.)

Here are the simple steps to deep relaxation, to dramatically lowering your energy level:

1. Get into a comfortable position. That is so obvious it needs no further description.
2. Make sure you have a quiet environment, a place where you won't be disturbed for the next 20 to 25 minutes.
3. You'll need a mental device, something upon which to concentrate that calls for your attention and narrows your focus. In some forms of meditation it is a word that is repeated, a mantra, such as, "Ommmm," or "One." In others it is something that is stared at, a mandala; or listened to, such as an audiotape, where you follow the voice on the tape (autogenic training). In others still, it is muscle groups that are tightened and released in sequence, starting at the head and working down to the toes, or vice versa (progressive relaxation).
4. Assume a passive attitude. One does not *try* to relax; one allows relaxation to occur. Thoughts, images, distractions come into your mind. Simply watch them float by, and refocus.

In Appendix A, I have given you a fully detailed relaxation exercise that you can record for yourself on an audiotape. The directions and the timing are all there; you can select your own background music. There are also many excellent relaxation tapes available in the market place; any good record store, bookstore, or health-food store will carry a wide selection.

It's important that you use a technique that is right for you. Some people find that listening to somebody else directing them goes against the grain. Others like that assistance, but eventually move to a tape of their favorite music while they supply their own inner script. Still others go to various centres that teach relaxation and meditation. In most North American cities, Buddhist temples, for example will teach you to meditate for little or no charge. I would strongly encourage you to investigate relaxation and to learn a technique. It will give you tremendous mental and physiological control over the impact of the high-paced environment in which we live.

CHAPTER SIX

Energy Management and Performance

High arousal and performance

You're playing cribbage with Art, my 75-year-old father-in-law, and after two hands you've taken a sizable lead. As he deals out the third hand, Art leans across the table and reminds you, with the wisdom of the ages, "The horse that craps fast doesn't crap long." Art's vocabulary hasn't improved much over the years, but his understanding of exercise physiology and its first principle is clear. Any marathon runner who does not manage his energy at the muscular level, who runs at a pace that is beyond what he is capable of doing for the first 20 miles, knows only too well what happens. He hits a wall, a physiological wall that neither courage, nor drive, nor stamina will get him through.

Learning to pace ourselves at the physiological level is essential in high-performance situations, but it is also critical to manage our mental energy. I'd like to tell you the story of an athlete who is not a gold-medal winner or world champion, but who nevertheless put in the performance of a lifetime. Elizabeth Manley won the silver medal in figure skating at the Calgary Olympics. (Many would argue that she deserved the gold.) She skated clean short and long programs landing five triples in her long program to gold medalist Katarina Witt's three.

I first met Elizabeth in 1984 after she'd been through some tough times. So intense were the stress and strain of competing at the top level of international figure skating that she'd suffered hair loss. In 1986 she lost the Canadian championship and went to the Geneva world championships as the number-two skater in the country. It's at this point that she began to truly study and apply the mental-fitness skills discussed in this book.

We spent a good deal of time working on the skills of positive self-talk and imagery. In Geneva she skated magnificently—clean short and long programs—and finished fifth in the world, the highest standing that she had achieved to that point. As she was now one of the top skaters in the world, she benefited from a European tour, where she had a chance to perform frequently and thereby improve her skills.

In Cincinnati in 1987 she finished third in the figures, skated an excellent short program, and was sitting fourth going into the long program. She had a shot at her dream— a medal. Her long program was a disaster. In examining that program afterward, she discovered that she had changed her goals and modified her usual way of approaching the program, because she so desperately wanted the gold medal. It was all she could think about. She suffered what is commonly known as "the choker's profile."

The lessons learned in Cincinnati contributed to her success at the 1988 Olympics. Despite the fact that she had a severe case of the flu and never did skate her complete program during the training sessions, she skated flawlessly in the figures and in the short and long programs. Her final performance was not one that anyone who saw it will soon forget. The applause was deafening. The medal was secondary; she had done what she had set out to do skate to the best of her ability in the Olympics and perform at a level where she had absolutely no regrets, knowing that she had gotten out all that she had within her.

Sports Illustrated and most other sport "authorities" did not predict a medal for Liz. They had seen in her a history of partial success and what they assumed was permanent "choking under intense pressure." There were many skills that she used to acquire the psychological edge that allowed her to achieve beyond what was expected of her. Most serious athletes will tell you (as have Michael Smith and Gaetan Boucher earlier in the book) that they acquire the physical skills long before they acquire the mental skills that allow them to perform at the highest level. By applying all of her skills, not only through the physical training that was necessary to get to her goal, but also through the mental training that is essential to success, Liz learned how not to sabotage her own performance.

The choker's profile

For the purpose of this discussion, we are going to use the word "arousal" to describe all forms of mental energy, positive or negative, be it enthusiasm, competiveness, anger, anxiety, excitedness. All of these raise our arousal level, and by doing so they narrow our attentional focus and lead to the choker's profile, which is the number-one performance problem not only in athletics, but also in most office, sales, job-interview, and home and parenting situations.

To examine how the choker's profile comes about, we're going to use a concept that was given to me years ago by Australian sports psychologist Brent Rushall. We're going to look at the relationship between our arousal level and our attentional focus. Often we talk about our attention being focused only on completing the sale, or winning the race, or disciplining the child, and so we blow it. However, the problem originates not with the wrong focus, but with our energy management. It's energy mismanagement, at the mental level, and inappropriate arousal level that leads to attentional problems. But let's start frrm the beginning.

TOTAL RELAXATION ———————————————————— **FIVE-FOOT-FLAME SYNDROME**

The preceding, terribly complicated diagram is an arousal-level scale. On one end we have total relaxation, that deep state that we achieve through mediation and relaxation, or that heavy state just before we fall asleep at night, where every once in a while our body twitches, but we're totally relaxed. At the extreme right is phenomenally high arousal—I'm so pumped up, so angry, so anxious, so competitive, whatever, that I have a five-foot flame coming out my back end. Now, an interesting thing happens as arousal level increases. When arousal level increases—that is, I move from left to right on the scale—attentional focus narrows. This process is depicted in the following diagram:

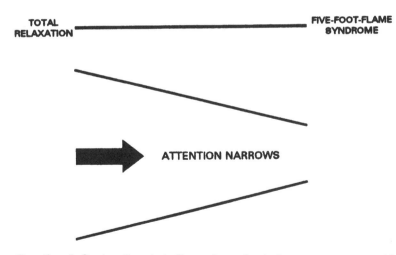

On the left, in the totally relaxed state, we can see that the attentional focus is broad; however, as we move across to the right hand side of the page, out attentional focus narrows and the lines get closer and closer. The number of items to which we can attend also decreases. Let's add some numbers to our chart to illustrate this relationship:

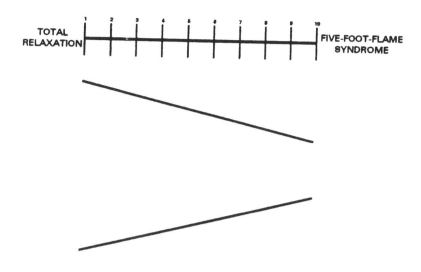

I've labeled the arousal-level scale from one to ten, one representing a highly relaxed state and ten representing a highly aroused state. These numbers do not translate literally into the number of items you can attend to at a particular arousal level; what I am trying to do here is give you a sense of the way arousal level inversely relates to attentional focus.

The defensive lineman can take an extremely high level of arousal because his task is simple. Leo Cahill probably put it best: "It's a very difficult job, being a defensive lineman— you take three steps and throw a fit." The quarterback, on the other hand, has a more complicated task and thus cannot take as high an arousal level. To repeat, if the skill component is simple and requires very little attention, we can take high-arousal levels.

But we're getting ahead of ourselves. We need to know two significant things before we can proceed: how skilled the performer is, and how difficult the task is. These are interrelated, as we shall see, but we will treat them separately at first. Let's assume that a certain task requires this much attention for Jamie.

The diagram below indicates that the arousal level that is ideal for Jamie's performance is at number three. When we slide Jamie's attentional requirements in our attentional shute, an ideal level of arousal for Jamie to still be able to pay attention to all the important facets of the task, yet be totally focused on performing the tasks, is a three—whatever three means to Jamie.

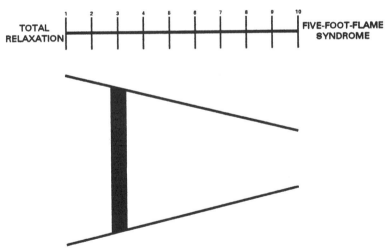

You can devise your own arousal-level scale from one to 10. You can go inside at key moments and decide the ideal level of arousal for the current situation, given past history. High-level performers know how to get themselves to exactly the right arousal level so that their attentional focus is 100 percent on what they're doing. If Jamie goes beyond his ideal arousal level to, say, an eight, this is what happens:

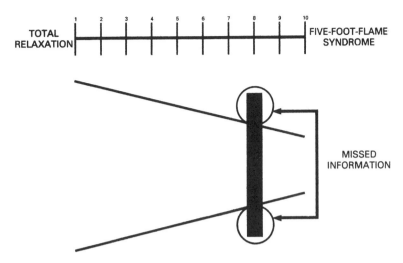

Certain important information falls outside Jamie's attentional scope. He is in what the coaches call the choker's profile—arousal level too high, given the skill level of the athlete or the complexity of the task. This results in one and the same thing: errors of underinclusion.

Complex tasks become simpler when they are well learned. A highly skilled performer can do a complicated task automatically and thus the task requires little attentional focus. The performer can sustain high arousal levels while performing. On the other hand, even a simple task, when it is first being learned, can be complicated. If we are too pumped up and aroused, learning becomes difficult, because we don't pay attention to all the things necessary to learn the task.

The last diagram is a typical illustration of the choker's profile. This could be the baseball player who tries to hit a home run instead of just trying to get on base when the team is down by three runs with no one on base in the bottom of the ninth inning. During the 1987 season, the Toronto Blue Jays lost all of their last seven games, eventually conceding the championship to Detroit by one game, and a good many of those by one run. Coming down the stretch they were missing two of their key players, Tony Fernandez and Ernie Whitt, both of whom were hurt.

George Bell (who was the Most Valuable Player in the American League that year) tried to carry the ball team; he tried to do it by himself. He tried to put the ball out of the ball park each time he came to bat. Manager Cito Gaston, when referring to that year, said "A normal George Bell would have won it for us. That's all we needed. We just needed him to do what he was capable of doing, nothing more."

Likewise, it could be the salesperson who goes into a meeting and talks the client into the product in the first five minutes and out of it in the next ten, because she was totally oblivious to the body language, questions, and vibrations coming from the customer. The sales rep is too pumped up while making the sale. This, by the way, can occur because she failed miserably in an earlier call and thus dramatically needed this next sale, thereby pushing her arousal level too high to perform well. Or perhaps she was brilliant in a previous call, which resulted in an unexpected sale and pushed her anticipation and eagerness to make the subsequent sale too high for optimum performance on the next call.

I've seen just as many athletes thrown off by brilliant performances in the first round as I have by miserable performances. Either instance has the same impact on the second round. In job interviews and performance appraisals, too high an arousal level leads to missing important information. If you come out of a meeting saying, "Gee when they said that, why didn't I say this?" and "I forgot to tell them this and this," it certainly isn't a question of not having the information. If you can think of what to say 30 seconds after you leave the situation, you know what you needed to know. Then why couldn't you get at it 30 seconds earlier, when you were in the situation? Well, your arousal level was too high, your attentional focus was too narrow, and you couldn't access the information.

We also see this when we look at management styles; too high an arousal level leads to making decisions that are based on what's happening at that moment and that have nothing to do with good long-term management. Ex-Yankee manager Billy Martin was noted for the quick starts his ball teams got, but he was also noted for the fact that his pitchers tended to get an inordinate number of arm problems late in the season. Managerial decisions made early in the season to win ball games didn't fit with good, long-range management. The desire to win led to a management style that missed important longer-range considerations.

Managers with a "kick-butt" style of management, who push for excellent month-end results, then spend two weeks trying to repair the relationships they've damaged, may be effective in the short term. But every month they have to start all over again, pushing and shoving to reach their objectives. In the long term they fail, because they haven't seen the long-range implications of their behavior in terms of the relationships, dedication, and commitment of their employees.

High-level performers, elite athletes, for example, can take potent arousal levels and still be highly successful, because their skills are so well learned. This is true of many great public speakers, as well. They can put high energy into their presentations because they know the material so well. Yo Yo Ma, the famous cellist, calls this "riding the edge." In an interview he talked about the importance of daring to go all the way to play with abandon—just on the edge where, if you go too far, you lose it. He was asked, "With such a difficult piece of music, don't you have to concentrate very hard on playing the piece technically?" He said, "Oh, no. If I start concentrating on that, I'm finished. I ride out to the edge and I play on the extreme edge of what I'm capable of doing."

High-level performers understand very well the limits of their arousal in reaching that ideal state. Steve Podborski, who is a former world downhill ski champion, talked about skiing down the hill relaxed and skiing down the hill pumped up. "Those were my bookends," he said. "I knew I had to reach a state somewhere between a seven and a seven and a half" (whatever a seven and a seven and a half meant to him). When Podborski was going up the lift, he went inside. "Where am I at right now? Mmm, I'm too high." And then he used breathing, relaxation, and imagery techniques to lower his arousal level. So it wasn't an accident that he was ready when he came down that hill.

High arousal, low-performance stories

My friend Jane told me an interesting story about her arousal level being too high and her performance low. She was working in a high-paced environment with a group of children, which required her to rush around the room trying to get everything done. When she went home, her husband Robert, said to her, "What happened to your legs?" She looked down, and her legs were completely covered with bruises and small cuts. She'd been knocking into tables and chairs, and hadn't even noticed that she had banged up her legs.

I had a gentleman named Scott in one of my workshops, who works as a manager of a large North American company. His first summer job as a university student was as a golf professional at a club in Vancouver, British Columbia. He had decided, in his words, that he was going to be "the greatest golf teacher ever." He was completely broke, so he arrived at work the first day hoping that he would find in his message slot a note to do a lesson or two. He looked into the slot and there was a slip of paper with the name of a Mr. Salmon and a phone number. He said, "I could see the $20 bill that I was going to earn, I wanted that money so badly. I was so hungry for it that my hands flew to the telephone dial. In fact, I stumbled over the telephone number several times in my anxiousness to reach Mr. Salmon." A young woman finally answered: "Vancouver Aquarium."

"Is Mr. Salmon there?" Scott said anxiously.

"No sir, you've reached the Vancouver Aquarium."

"Look," he said, "I've got to speak to Mr. Salmon. A Mr. Salmon has phoned. He wants a golf lesson."

And for five minutes he insisted on talking to Mr. Salmon, until finally the young lady hung the phone up in exasperation. When he turned around the three other golf professionals were holding their sides and rolling on the floor with laughter. His high arousal level had narrowed his attentional focus to the point where he could not link the Vancouver Aquarium and Mr. Salmon with a practical joke.

Mickey Mantle tells a great story about Billy Martin and himself when they played years ago with the Yankees. On an off day one Fall, they drove three and a half hours to the farm of a friend of Mantle's to go hunting. They arrived at 7:30 in the morning, having arisen before 4:00 a.m., and Mantle left Martin in the pickup truck while he talked to his friend in the farmhouse to see where they might hunt without endangering any of the men working on the farm. The friend told Mantle where he could hunt and asked him if he would do a favor for him: would he please go and shoot a mule, a family pet that had gone lame and blind in its fifteenth year. Would he please put the mule out of its misery.

Mantle, at first, was reluctant to do this, but finally agreed. On his way down the farmhouse steps to the pickup truck, he decided to pull Martin's leg a bit. He got into the truck, pounded the steering wheel, and said in an upset tone, "Unbelievable!" Martin asked him what was wrong, and Mantle said they couldn't hunt there. Martin, his arousal level rising instantly, demanded, "Why not?" and insisted on speaking to the farmer. Mantle said, "No way," and started to drive into the farmyard.

Martin demanded, "Where are we going?"

Mantle said, "We are going to shoot his mule."

"You can't shoot a man's mule," said Martin.

"Oh, yeah?" said Mantle. "Watch this!"

Mantle got out of the vehicle and dropped the mule in one shot, thankful that he had gotten this unpleasant task over with. As he turned to get back into the vehicle, heard several loud noises. He looked around and saw Martin standing outside the truck with his gun smoking. "What are you doing?" Mantle asked.

"I got two of his cows," replied Martin.

High arousal clearly leads to a narrow attentional focus that leads to poor performance and, in this instance, dead cattle.

Moment-to-moment skills to lower arousal level

Awareness

Until we become aware that we are mismanaging our energy level, we will not be able to make dramatic adjustments to our performance level. There's little you can do about the clothes you are wearing, or your personality, five minutes before walking into a job interview, a performance appraisal, or a presentation. But, right there in that hallway before walking in for your performance, you can go inside yourself and check your inner or mental readiness. You can do an attitude check: "How positive am I feeling?" You can also do an altitude check: "Where's my energy level? Am I too high? Too low? Where was I the last time I was in a situation similar to this and performed well? I'd say I was at about a six last time, and I'm at about an eight this time." Then take the next two or three minutes to lower your arousal level. You might, for example, use the centering technique, described later in the chapter. You might also engage in some self-talk. You might practice an affirmation. You might use imagery, which we'll discuss later in this book. Remember what I said at the outset: all of the skills you are learning work interdependently.

Perception

Do a perception check. You may find that the way you are looking at an upcoming event is increasing your arousal level. Perhaps you can reframe the event. Perhaps you can change your view of it. Some other perception that you are carrying around with you at this moment may be putting a lot of pressure on you. The athlete who quickly recognizes, a couple of minutes before the meet, that this meet is just "going to school," it's just a preparation event, goes a long way toward managing his arousal level. Likewise, an entrant in the Olympics may recognize that the competition is only one thing she is going to do in her life, thereby gaining some perspective that allows her to manage her energy.

I work with a hurdler who trains in California who has 10 hurdles in her race. She gradually learned to add one more hurdle mentally as she trained for the Olympic Games. She had started out trying to be perfect over one hurdle. In fact, she had treated that hurdle as the final tape, because she was working on leaning into it as she went over it. But slowly, as if they were chapters in a book, she added another hurdle—chapter two, then chapter three, and so on. Finally, the whole "book" was completed for the summer Olympics. At that point, she realized that this particular "book," this set of hurdles, was not really a whole story, but part of a broader story, a chapter in her whole life. This outlook allowed her to decrease the pressure that she felt at the Olympics. She recognized that this was just one small part of the whole that is her life.

Retracing

Sometimes you may notice that your energy level is inappropriately high, but there doesn't seem to be anything apparent causing your anxiety. Retrace your day to figure out where it happened. "I was okay at lunch. Oh, the argument I had after lunch with my spouse. That's still bothering me as I head into this meeting. Ah!" Retracing allows you to get in touch with what caused the feelings, and that awareness alone can diminish your arousal to a more appropriate level. It also allows you to quickly decide what to do with that awareness right now. "I'll call afterward and work it out." You can park the problem, or release it—skills that we'll discuss in the chapter on Imagery.

Use a miniskill

There are many miniskills available to us. Here are a few adapted from various sources:

- **The breath counter:** Sit comfortably in a quiet place, back straight, feet flat on the floor, hands in your lap. Count the inhalation of each breath mentally: "inhale...one, inhale...two, inhale...three, inhale..four..." Hold each breath for a few seconds, then slowly release the air to the count of eight. You should take twice as long to exhale as you do to inhale. Inhale through your nose and exhale through your mouth. Try not to lose your count. If you do, or you find yourself thinking about anything except the act of breathing and the number of that breath, refocus on your breathing, returning to "inhale...one," if necessary. Thoughts will intrude, but just let them pass by and refocus on your breathing. With practice, concentrating on your breath will become easy.
- **Walking as if you have time:** Walk slowly, focusing on your breath. Begin each inhalation with "in," and each exhalation with "out." Then count each step as you walk and breathe, so that mentally you are saying, "In, two, three, four,...out, two, three, four..." or perhaps "in, two, three,...out, two, three." Continue to substitute "in" or "out" for each count of "one." According to your own breathing pattern, your exhalations may be longer than your inhalations, or vice versa. Just breathe, walk, and count, getting in rhythm with you own breath, and keep consistent. Your mind will wander. Gently bring it back. You'll arrive at your next meeting more relaxed and ready to deal with whatever awaits.

Centering

One technique for lowering arousal level is a breathing technique called centering. The beauty of breathing techniques, of course, is that they're unobtrusive. Everybody expects you to breathe (in fact, if you don't breathe for an extended period of time when you're with a group, it really throws them off). No one knows you are using centering. Here are the steps involved:

- Check your neck and shoulder muscles for tension.
- Reduce the tension in your jaw.
- Put 100 percent of your attention into your breathing and inhale slowly from down in your diaphragm.
- Let the air out and shift your attention to your shoulders (release) and knees (bend) or, it seated, buttocks (press down).
- Repeat if necessary.

I know professional golfers who use centering on the tour. Akido masters use it when defending themselves against unexpected attacks from anywhere in a horseshoe of opponents. Public speakers use it when they are challenged with a difficult question. The Workers' Compensation Board Downsview Rehabilitation Clinic in Toronto teaches centering to patients who are dealing with phantom-limb pain after an amputation. They call it a "minitranquilizer," and it is just that; it's a marvelous, moment-to-moment energy-management skill.

When you are stuck in traffic you have two choices— learn to fly or deal with the situation. What a wonderful opportunity to use the centering technique. When you're being challenged by one of your children, what a wonderful opportunity to use centering to lower your arousal level so that you can summon all your parenting skills at that moment. When you go into a highly critical meeting to present something that is very near and dear to you, and right off the bat it feels as though your point is being challenged, centering is an excellent skill to lower your arousal level, gain a broader perspective, and maintain the poise that you need.

Centering is a multilevel, multidimensional skill. Once you learn it, you'll realize it's doing a lot more than you first imagined. There's a clear message at the body level and at the feeling level. Combine centering with an affirmation as you complete the release of the air, and you can move to a calmer place mentally very quickly. *But, like all other skills, it has to be practiced; it has to be used in order to be maintained.* Try using the centering technique five to ten times a day. Place Post-it Notes on the dashboard of your car or on your telephone to remind you. After a period of two or three weeks, you will see a return on your investment.

Low arousal and performance

Have you ever had one of those flat, unmotivated days when you're sitting around the office looking at all the people behind their desks, and you say to yourself, "How could one organization have hired so many slugs?" You think about how you've really got to get to bed at a decent time that night. You have a lot of work to do, but you just can't get into it. Then the telephone rings, and on the other end of the line is a friend who brings out the best in you, whom you haven't heard from in a long time. He says, "I'm in town. Let's get together. I'll see you after work." You hang up the phone; 30 seconds have gone by. Your energy level's up; you're positive; you greet people in the office; you get down to work. What's changed? Have brain transplants been administered in the office? Have you had 10 hours of sleep? What's changed is your energy level. You've been energized. Now, if you can get someone who has such a positive influence to phone you at all the critical points of your life, you probably won't need any of the information or skills that follow. But maybe you need to learn how to phone yourself.

Let's look at that low arousal level in terms of our diagram. Let's assume that Jamie is about to do a task that's been done a thousand times before, and therefore, that task only requires a certain amount of attention. When we slide that into our diagram, it looks like this:

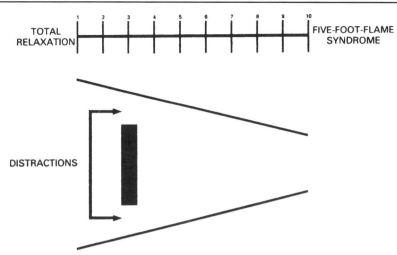

You can see that Jamie's arousal level is only at a three, and therefore he has all kinds of attention left over. Jamie is not totally immersed in the task. A flat, rambling, uninvolved, off-the-topic performance is the result. Jamie makes errors of overinclusion, noticing everything that is happening. He includes too much information in the process of doing the task and takes twice the amount of time to do the job, because he is not involved in it. Jamie needs to move his arousal level up. He needs to energize.

Energizing

Our energy level involves our body—our physiology and our actions—but it also involves our thoughts and feelings. Jamie may feel tired at the physiological level because he needs sleep, fluids, or nutritious food—the most important long-term solutions to maintaining high energy levels physically. Or he may not feel like getting involved; the task may bore him. He may not be able to change how he feels about the task, but he can, in the short term, change what he is thinking or doing. This will have an effect on his feelings and his physiology.

Cal Botterill, a well-known Canadian sports psychologist, wrote a comprehensive article on techniques for energizing in a Canadian coaching journal. He listed energizing tips—things you can do and think to increase arousal level. Some of his suggestions included exercise, stretching with deep breathing, visualizing yourself setting aside feelings of fatigue and then immersing yourself in some physical activity that fully demands your attention (like juggling or bouncing a ball off your foot). Interacting with others in a positive way can affect your energy level. A shower or massage can produce feelings of regeneration, readiness, and responsiveness. Music and videotapes can energize, depending on their style and content, which are obviously matters of personal choice.

Botterill said that it is important to monitor your thoughts, particularly your imagery, in order to maintain mental energy. Choose thoughts and images that evoke feelings of energy within you. For example, see yourself accomplishing your goals—imagine yourself skiing down an exciting hill (if you're a skier, that is). Focus on highly energized images that have meaning for you. I often think of an intense, vibrant stream of light entering my body and flowing to all parts of my being, energizing me as it moves. Think of an animal that symbolizes power and energy, or a force in nature that signifies power to you. Focus your self-talk on phrases and cue words that energize you, or use a slogan or affirmation that makes you feel alive. Draw on the energy of others around you; imagine a tube connecting you to them and feel the energy exchange. Channel your feelings into a transformer and watch them come out as positive, vital feelings. You can gain control over how you feel by choosing what you think, imagine, and do.

Learning how to assess your energy level and identify energy blocks such as boredom and fatigue are critical skills. Once you do, you can begin to use techniques to counteract or compensate for energy drains. Monitoring and evaluating the effectiveness of your techniques will be important to your overall success in creating and maintaining a high level of energy at will.

A final word on energy management

It's unfortunate that it often takes a tragedy to remind us that we should live and enjoy each day. By choosing to be more aware every day of our lives, by selecting perceptions that are realistic and life enhancing, we can manage our energy levels more efficiently. Learning to regulate our energy levels will assist us in preparing for critical events and key performances, and we will perform better. But the real return on managing our energy is long-term health and well-being. That's the real payoff.

CHAPTER SEVEN

Attentional Skills

*But how can I know when my attention has
wandered...when I need my attention to
find it?*

—Frustrated athlete in
conversation with the author

Perhaps no other area captures the attention of business
executives attending my workshop as vividly as attentional
skills. When I ask why participants have come to the workshop, a large percentage make reference to attention. Some
typical self-assessments include:

"I've got to learn to concentrate better."

"I lose my focus."

"I react to changes without thinking enough."

"I've got to learn to focus on my message, rather than on
my fears."

"I'd like to read the audience better."

"I'd like to be able to reduce the distractions that interfere
with my listening."

"I'd like to be able to tell which one of my 'team members'
will stick to the game plan too long and which one will
change at every juncture."

On the surface, the concept of attention appears to be
something of a contradiction. You *are* paying attention when
you're daydreaming—if your intention is to do some creative
problem solving—but if you're in the middle of a business

meeting, you've got the wrong attentional focus. Every form of attention has its place, and the key, as we shall see, is the congruency between the demands of the situation and the attentional style you bring to it.

In a study of 1984 Olympic athletes, sports psychologists Terry Orlick and John Partington found that one of the major problems for those who did not perform at their expected level was that they were "blown away" by distractions. The athletes were prepared for the physical performance, but they were not prepared for the multitude of distractions they had to face in competition. Their focus was everywhere but on the task at hand. Orlick and Partington suggested that athletes needed a plan to deal with distractions. Part of that planning process, of course, is having a clear understanding of the possible distractions at a competitive event and the kind of focus that will get the best results given the task to be performed.

Attentional focus

The first step to understanding attentional focus, as with each skill set we've discussed, is to develop a vocabulary that allows us to describe more accurately the concept of

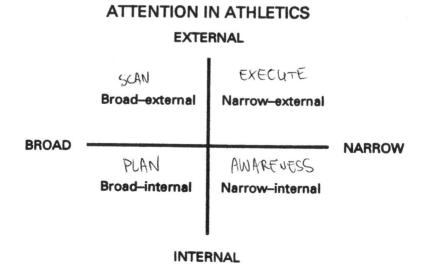

ATTENTION IN ATHLETICS

EXTERNAL

SCAN	EXECUTE
Broad–external	**Narrow–external**

BROAD ———————————————— NARROW

PLAN	AWARENESS
Broad–internal	**Narrow–internal**

INTERNAL

"paying attention." Robert Nideffer, the world-renowned San Diego sports psychologist, developed an excellent conceptual framework that, despite its simplicity, brings accuracy and vivid clarity to an analysis of attentional skills. His model, summarized in the diagram on the previous page, may look anything but simple at first. But stick with me on this. If I've worked it easily into my everyday vocabulary, it'll be a snap for you.

The first axis of attention is width. It can be broad or narrow. I can include lots of data (broad) or just one piece of information (narrow). The second axis is that of direction. My attention can be focused in one of two possible directions: internal (my thoughts, feelings, an idea, something inside me), or external (the room, my daughter building a sand castle, the tennis ball I'm about to return).

There are four quadrants created through the crossing of these two axes, corresponding to four attentional styles:

- **Broad-external:** indicates that a person can deal with and react to a breadth of external stimuli in an effective manner.
- **Broad-internal:** indicates that a person is able to concentrate and integrate input when many things are happening at once, or when there's a lot of information to integrate and to draw conclusions from.
- **Narrow-external:** indicates a person who is able to concentrate effectively on a single object or source of information externally, such as hitting a baseball or focusing on a speaker.
- **Narrow-internal:** indicates that a person is able to concentrate effectively on what goes on within. This is synonymous with the concept of awareness.

In the chapter on Energy Management, we mentioned that there is a width dimension to attention: it can be broad, or it can be narrow. With a broad attentional focus, I see everything in the room. With a narrow attentional focus, I see only this word, *narrow*. It's the difference between a wide-angle and a zoom lens.

German sports psychologist Frank Schubert had an interesting way of conceptualizing attention. He said to visualize your concentration as a spotlight.

> There is a spotlight in your head, and you are the lighting crew, cameraman, and director. The beam of light from the spotlight—your attention—can bathe everything you desire in its glowing light. If it is focused on one object in particular, it will light up brilliantly, with everything around it fading into the darkness [the equivalent of Nideffer's narrow attentional focus]. But if you open up the aperture in front of the spotlight, the beam of light will be less concentrated. Thus, several objects can be lit, although not as brightly as before.

This, he said, is your ability to broaden your attentional style.

Which points to another critical dimension of attention: the ability to shift styles. If you are an experienced "cameraman," in a fraction of a second you can light up one corner of a business meeting with one small, narrow beam of light, yet quickly back up, open the aperture, and shed your focus on the whole room. We will get to the ability to shift attentional focus later in the chapter.

The last of Dr. Nideffer's concepts that we will introduce here is his concept of overload. The idea of overload helps to differentiate between appropriate and inappropriate attentional styles. If I use an attentional style that is inappropriate, I am in attentional overload in that style. If, for example, I'm trying to hit a tennis ball (narrow-external focus required), but at the same time I'm mentally analyzing my stroke, or if I'm daydreaming when I'm supposed to be finishing my report (narrow-internal/external focus required), I am in the wrong attentional focus. In both instances, I am overloaded in broad-internal. Great thinkers are great when thinking is required, but they're locked in a lousy frame of mind when it comes to hitting a baseball.

Many of us have a favorite style that we use repeatedly, even if it's inappropriate. Some of us are analytical (broad-internal), for example, and we use that focus even in situations where another focus would be more appropriate. Once we become aware of what style, or styles, in which we tend to overload, we can begin to establish an attentional plan that helps us stay focused. I know, for example, that I have trouble in the narrow attentional focus on occasion. If, for instance, I'm in a room where the TV is turned on and I'm trying to carry on a conversation, the TV constantly distracts me (external overload). I will make eye contact, go back to the TV, make eye contact, go back to the TV. This, of course, presents me with many options as a performer, one of which is to go over and turn the TV off. But we will get to solutions later.

In times of stress, we often automatically go to our favorite attentional style. And, as we learned in the chapter on Energy Management, pressure can affect our attention. Increased arousal level narrows our attentional focus. Even great thinkers, when stressed, can miss information they would normally acquire if they become narrow and focused on too few things, thereby making errors of underinclusion.

Many of the athletes I work with take their normal everyday attentional style to their sport with disastrous results, particularly those who are very good students. They are so adept at the broad-internal, or analytical, style that they don't react quickly enough to move out of this style when necessary in their sport. Deadlines for university term papers allow four times the amount of time necessary to do the project properly, and if you bring the broad-internal attentional style required for writing essays to the sporting world, you are not going to react and move quickly enough from style to style. The broad-internal style is often ineffective in the business world, too, because you just don't have the kind of time you had in university to prepare reports, particularly when suddenly, without warning, a surprise project lands on your desk.

Nideffer developed a comprehensive questionnaire called T.A.I.S. (Test of Attentional and Interpersonal Style), which I've used with thousands of athletes and business-people over the past 10 years. Being aware of personal over-load areas is valuable in learning to stay focused on the task at hand, but we don't really need to write the test of atten-tional style here to improve our understanding of attention. What about you? What are your attentional strengths and problem areas? Are you distracted more by thoughts and feelings (internal), or by everyday events around you (exter-nal)? Do you become distracted by a single obsessive thought, perhaps something that happened at work, that keeps you focused narrowly on things not in your immedi-ate environment (narrow-internal)? Or are you paralyzed by analysis, the broad-internal style, when there's a complicat-ed sequence of events to sort out, or too many "to do's" in your attentional lens. Overload in the broad-internal style can also be caused just by having too much information to process; we are too busy and we have too many things screaming for our attention.

Improving your attentional skills

We have several options when planning to improve atten-tional skills:

1. Design the event out.
   If, in any way, you can design the event out—that is, get rid of the distraction—do so. Turn off the television. Close the door.
2. Develop a strategy.
   Become aware. Make a choice. Act.
3. Have a distraction plan.
   Have a series of skills that you can call on to refocus your attention when you find yourself distracted.

Awareness is the first mental skill we apply in our strategy to improve our attentional focus. We first have to notice that our attention has been distractive before we can do something to redirect to the task at hand. Often we don't know our attention has wandered and that we've lost 10 to 15 minutes in reverie. Unless we've checked exactly what the time is before we start something, we won't know that we've been caught daydreaming.

To ensure that we stay focused through a particular phase or event, it is also essential to keep in mind one other factor: we cannot maintain a highly concentrated intensity over a long period of time. The higher the intensity of concentration required, the shorter it can be maintained. It's important that we design a plan that allows us periods of reduced focus whenever possible. It doesn't mean that we fall asleep, but that in certain situations we back down, like a soccer goaltender who cannot concentrate at 100-percent intensity all of the time. When his team is playing the ball, he relaxes his concentration a bit, and then, as his opponents approach him with the ball from the other end of the field, he begins to get narrower and more focused.

In meetings, there are times when we can reduce our energy level, thus broadening our attentional focus to take in general information in a more relaxed fashion, then increase the intensity of our concentration to a narrower focus when we need to. In sport this is called "playing within yourself," being able to relax and back off, yet stay focused at a high intensity for short bursts when that is absolutely necessary. More experienced players are able to maintain high-focused attention for a longer period of time than their less experienced counterparts. When athletes make more errors in the second half of a game than in the first half, it's not because of the players' fitness, which is easily tested, but often because they were not concentrating to the extent that they were earlier. It may be that they burned themselves out attentionally in the first half, or that they just need some additional skills that will allow them to narrow and stay focused at the appropriate times in the second half of the game.

I cannot function at a high intensity level day after day, week after week, or eventually I'll burn myself out. Think again of Frank Schubert's analogy of the spotlight. Intelligent business people, like intelligent athletes, know when they have to turn the light on bright and narrow, and when they can turn it down. Once we can start to think this way, it is much easier to design a plan. The first step in developing a strategy, as we have said, is awareness. With a new vocabulary and way of looking at attention, we can gain enough awareness to catch ourselves when we're inappropriately focused, and thus be able to make necessary changes in focus.

What about deadlines? Are they distractions, or do they often work to help us focus on the task? As I wrote this book, I had to create many "false" deadlines for myself, because without a deadline I know that I don't stay focused and narrow on a task. I would have kept adding to the material and would never have completed the book. To quote Samuel Johnson, "When a man knows he is to be hanged in a fortnight, it concentrates his mind wonderfully." When we are extremely busy, however, deadlines can operate as distractions.

The next step is to make a choice, to choose an action. It may be reframing. When she was asked, "What would you do if you were more tired than usual before an event?" Linda Thom, a gold-medal winner in pistol shooting at the Los Angeles Olympics, replied that she would simply say to herself, "This could be to my advantage. I'll be calmer; control will be easier." Reframing often helps us stay on track. Anxiety, after all, is just misplaced attention.

"The mind," said Lao-tzu, the Chinese philosopher, "is like an untrained horse. It runs everywhere." When your mind gets used to wandering, it becomes good at wandering. But there are several things that you can do to improve your ability to concentrate. One is to demand of yourself consistency, even in minor situations, to keep control of your attention. Some athletes maintain accurate daily logs of their ability to pay attention through certain sections of a performance. That's advisable for anyone trying to increase her ability to pay attention over a longer period of time. Even the smallest tasks should not be done inattentively; keep your attention focused on the results at hand when you are actually performing. This means, of course, that you must want to improve your attentional ability. Linda Thom highly recommends video games to increase powers of concentration. "You really have to concentrate on them," she says, "or you lose."

Another way to improve your ability to concentrate is to make dull exercises more exciting. Add some vitality and zest to them. Make them interesting and challenging, or they're not worth concentrating on. Unusual or striking situations or objects attract your attention automatically. As a business person, challenge yourself to look for something different as you do a familiar task. Become a detective; find something unique or different. Use the analogy of the spotlight. You'll be surprised what you find of interest by varying your work and the way you work. But please remember that physical fatigue will dramatically affect how much attention you can pay to specific things over long periods of time.

The distraction plan

Most high performers in all walks of life have a distraction plan. They plan the work and then they work the plan. In the chapter on Mental Preparation, we will describe in detail what goes into a good, strong mental-preparation plan. Here it will suffice to say that the single most effective way of dealing with potential attentional problems is to know what to expect and to plan ahead for potential distractions. Linda Thom says:

I don't come in with blinkers on, and I don't come in deliberately looking around. I want to be aware of the things I need to be aware of and avoid distracting myself with things that don't matter. I get to the site at least half an hour before the competition so I can have all variables in hand. Are things on schedule? Are the officials in place? Has anything changed? Is the equipment working? And how is the light and the weather vis-à-vis the targets? I calmly observe these and many other things, although in some instances this is done peripherally. Then I park them out of the way and pay attention to what I want to do—to follow my plan.

A distraction plan involves applying the skills we learned earlier to the area of attention. Imagery, which we will discuss in greater detail in the next chapter, is probably the most obvious skill to apply. Parking, or setting aside, irrelevant thoughts or concerns and refocusing our attention allow us to get on with what we are doing. Linda Thom talks about "snipping." She says that she's learned to deal with negative thoughts by cutting them off. "I notice the distant, early-warning signs of a negative thought and I cut it off as early as I can. When you learn to do this, you can snip off the thought before it can disturb you." She says out loud, "Cut that out! Stop!" and combines this with a body message, nodding to reward herself for recognizing it—not shaking her head, which is a negative act.

Lanny Bassham, 1976 gold medalist in the smallbore three-position rifle, talks about dealing with the problems of analyzing performance too much. "I don't want to know how I shot an eight. I want to know how I will shoot this next 10." He knows he can't afford to get involved in paralysis by analysis, thinking while shooting. Analysis, the broad-internal focus, is fine, but it's for after the competition, not during it. When some athletes find themselves being distracted by analysis, or judging, they simply say to themselves,

"Analyze, analyze, analyze," or "Judge, judge, judge," making a joke of it, then they refocus where they want to be.

Bassham uses self-talk to stay focused. Self-talk can also assist us by giving us something to focus on. Most great performers use cue words that scream for their attention at difficult junctures. Some gymnasts follow an attentional script, which is especially strong in areas of their program where they might be distracted. We, in our everyday work life, can use attentional scripts that keep us focused and call for our attention. Sometimes it means talking out loud, saying, "Okay now, do this and get it done within the next five minutes. Follow these four steps: number one, check this out; number two, call the marketing department; number three..." and so on. We increase our ability to focus and apply our will when we have an attentional script of cue words that demand our attention.

Let's suppose that I'm sitting at my desk, trying to write a report, but my mind is wandering. I notice, when I choose to become aware, that I am focusing on something that I have coming up down the road—an important meeting. Being aware of this allows me to do several things. If I'm putting too much pressure on myself concerning this meeting, I might reframe it to give it less importance and put it in perspective. I might park it and say, "All right, obviously you want my attention, so on the way home in the car this afternoon I will carefully go over my preparation for that meeting." I will get perspective quickly, because I have become aware and chosen to do something about it.

I might then run an image of myself working efficiently for the rest of the afternoon focused on getting the report done, seeing myself during the first 10 minutes laying it out and planning how I want to write it. Then I might see myself getting up for a cup of coffee, greeting people, but not being too distracted by them (this is my attentional break, like the goal tender in the soccer game), then coming back, closing my door to shut out distractions. I, for one, definitely have to do this; otherwise, I end up carrying on conversations from my desk with people out in the hall, because I become so overloaded by what happens around me. I'll be trying to write a report at the same time as I'm yelling out corrections in the conversation: "No, the meeting isn't at seven—it's at eight o'clock."

Some people might say, "It's nice that you have that plan, but I don't notice when I'm distracted. My mind is wandering all over the place. How do I find my attention, when I need my attention to find my wandering attention?"

There are several ways that you can check to see whether you're in the right attentional framework for what you're doing. One way is to put five or six pieces of masking tape around your home to act as cues for attentional checks. Let's assume, for example, that you're shaving or putting on your makeup in the morning and you look up and notice a piece of tape hanging from the mirror. You ask yourself two questions. First, "What attentional framework was I in? Oh, gee, I was analyzing all the things I have to do today and putting too much pressure on myself." Second, "What attentional framework should I be in? I should be in narrow, finishing what I am doing here and getting out of the house." You can catch yourself and make a shift to get back on track.

You can also do the same thing by putting a piece of masking tape on your watch, so that every time you look at your watch, it reminds you to check your attentional style and redirect it if necessary. Or you can set the beeper on your watch. This may sound a little juvenile, but a good many of the performers I have worked with have used these techniques with great success. They were amazed at how much time they were losing because their mind was somewhere else rather than where it should have been.

If I'm engrossed in deep analysis (broad-internal) before walking into an important meeting, it's difficult to move instantly to the narrow-external attentional style necessary to make my points at that meeting. There is little guarantee, if I am considering all sorts of doubts and information, that I will be precise, concise, and narrow. This, of course, is most evident in the laboratory of sport, where, if an athlete's attention wanders for a second, everybody knows it, because he's made a mistake. I can't be analyzing in the on-deck circle and narrow and focused in the batter's box. The transition is too difficult to make. Elite athletes warm up the attentional style that they will need for their event by starting to get into that style at least five to ten minutes before they enter the performance arena. Just as Michael Smith said in chapter two: "When I'm down to two guys ahead of me, I start thinking about the jump. When I'm down to the last guy, I'm ready. I'm on the runway centered and focused, before he's off."

There's nothing to stop us from doing this, too. I can make sure that I have rehearsed the way I want to be and act in a meeting. When I understand what is required of a situation—how I tend to be distracted and how to deal with those distractions—I can rehearse those requirements, thereby ensuring that I'm attentionally "warmed up" for the task.

If I have a tendency, for example, to overload in external, to be distracted by things in my environment when I am speaking to someone (perhaps in a sales situation), I can make sure that I put my back to the distraction. This is not difficult to do. If I'm sitting at someone's desk and there are distractions on the other side of that desk, I can turn my chair slightly sideways and maintain eye contact with the person while cutting out many of the distractions.

If I tend to overload in the broad-internal style, and I need to be clear and precise for a presentation, then I must plan. I must have an attentional script that keeps me focused, step by step, on what I'm going to do in that presentation. I have to see myself staying on time. I have to envisage all the red herrings that might throw me off, or as many as I can, and have clear ideas about how to deal with them. If, on the other hand, I have a tendency to get narrow and stuck on one thing, putting myself in danger of missing the forest for the trees, I need to ensure that I manage my energy during that meeting. I must stay relaxed, broaden the spotlight, and be able to see with a new perspective.

We can also plan for the attentional style of those we are going to meet. We all know people, for instance, who are distracted by the sights and sounds around them. They try to make eye contact, but they're distracted by people walking behind them, or by noises in the next office. They are constantly turning their heads and then having to pull their attention back to the matter at hand. Working with the management division of a large organization, I suggested role-playing some attentional problems and solutions. One person was role-playing a performance appraisal with a boss who was extremely distracted. She elected to go ahead of time to the restaurant where she was going to meet him to get a secluded table in the back. She talked to the waiter to ensure that there would not be a lot of interruptions. She sat with her back to the wall with her boss facing her, so that all he could see was her and the wall.

On sales calls with customers who are unfocused because of constant interruptions, is there a way to ensure that the client stays narrow and focused on what you're saying? You could ask the client to meet elsewhere, or suggest, "Rather than taking an hour, why don't we take five minutes of really one-on-one, face-to-face communication, because neither of us has time to waste. Let's get it all done and get out of here." If you know, on the other hand, that the person gets narrow and stuck on price, procedure, or past events, then you need to reframe from a broader perspective constantly as you go through your presentation.

A plan that all parties can refer to enhances attentional focus. In meetings, for example, having a clear agenda is essential to staying in focus and on track. Knowing ahead of time what time the meeting will finish keeps people wonderfully focused.

I'm sure you see that the skills involved in self-talk, energy management, and imagery can be used to redirect attention that has wandered. But, as in all of these skills, awareness is the foundation. The key is to become aware when we are distracted, either through analysis of past performance, or by catching ourselves the instant our attentional style becomes inappropriate, then using a skill to redirect ourselves to get back on track.

More exercises to improve concentration

What follows are some attentional exercises that you can use to increase your ability to concentrate. They're adapted from *Red Gold*, the Soviet book on sports psychology, as well as from several other sources:

Handling situation overload

When you find yourself totally overloaded, try any one of these four techniques:

- Change your environment. Go somewhere quiet where you can concentrate.
- Screen out the irrelevant, change seats, remove all unnecessary distractions from your field of vision.
- Practice centering or releasing to calm yourself.
- Step back—physically. Take a deep breath or a few deep breaths and then go back to your task.

Concentration control

Here are a few techniques to develop concentration:

- **Tuning in/tuning out:** Read a book while the news is on the radio. Alternate your attention in 20-second intervals between reading and listening, then try to become oblivious to what you're reading while you are listening, and vice versa. Do this for about five minutes every day until you reach your objective: total concentration on reading to the total exclusion of the news.
- **Just one more time:** If several people are talking to you at the same time, choose which one to listen to and block out the competing voices.

- **Concentration—count on it:** Learn to become an introvert at will. Imagine turning the beam of your attention inward. While the news is still on the radio, start subtracting in your mind the number seven from 100, and keep subtracting by sevens. Do this exercise daily, until you can become oblivious to the news while subtracting.

Mindfulness training

Here are two excellent techniques to bring your level of arousal down, increase your concentration, and intensify attention to detail:

- **Time ticks:** Sit down by yourself in a room and stare at the second hand of your watch for one minute. See how long you can maintain the following thought: I am sitting here looking at the hand of the watch. Count how many times your mind veers from this thought. Repeat this exercise for three minutes every day until you are able to keep your mind completely on this single thought.
- **Breathing here and now:** Sit in a chair, with both feet on the ground, arms uncrossed. Close your eyes, take a deep breath, and let it out slowly as you begin to relax from the forehead downward... Once you are relaxed, notice your breathing and, without changing its rhythm, begin to count silently so that one breath (in and out) counts as one, the next inhalation and exhalation counts as two, and so on. When you reach 10, go back to one and start again. If you lose count or find yourself counting beyond 10, stop and trace your wandering thoughts back as far as you can. Start again at one. To begin with, about five to eight minutes of this exercise is enough.

The people who go through my workshops tell me that having a way to talk about attention (broad or narrow, external or internal) not only makes the concept clear, it dramatically increases their awareness of when and in which situations they are off base attentionally. Just having a way of observing helps us notice and redirect our focus on a day-to-day, moment-to-moment basis.

If I catch myself distracted by people or store windows in a mall, I label that focus— "overload external, Peter"—congratulate myself for catching it, and refocus on why I came to the mall in the first place. I find all kinds of time that used to be lost. By reminding myself of my intended focus before I write a report, speak to an audience, listen to my son's request, I'm much more effective in what I'm doing.

There are days, however, when I choose to watch what is happening around me. I choose to get lost in the passing scene. I love to watch people, people with people, people performing, people creating, people being people—I call it applied research.

CHAPTER EIGHT

Imagery

Imagination is more important than knowledge.
> —Albert Einstein

What you see is what you get.
> —Flip Wilson as "Geraldine"

Captain Gerald Coffey was an excellent golfer, so it wasn't surprising for him to shoot an 84. What was surprising was that he shot 84 in his first round of golf after spending seven years as a prisoner of war in Vietnam. Although he left that horrendous environment weighing only 130 pounds, in his first round of golf back in the United States it was as if he hadn't suffered the trauma of incarceration. Indeed, it seemed as if he hadn't been away from the game at all. When asked how he did this, he replied that he had played golf every single day in the Vietnamese prisoner-of-war camp. He had played all kinds of golf courses, hole by hole, in his mind.

During the intermission of a CBS-televised concert from New York's Lincoln Center two years ago, conductor David Zinman and cellist Yo Yo Ma discussed the use of imagery in their performances. They spoke of using visual clues, such as "seeing that note." To get the proper touch in the finale of a piece, they said they held in their minds the image of an ash slowly growing and bending at the end of a cigarette. In considering a Tchaikovsky symphony, Yo Yo Ma turned to

Zinman and said, "What was the image we used, remember, when we played that piece in London?" Zinman replied, "A greased dove against a bleak gray sky." Now, that image may not mean a lot to you, because it's not your image. To Zinman and Ma, however, it expressed the mood they wanted to conjure up for the audience.

The language of imagery can create within us mood and feeling, as it does for the musicians, or it can reinforce physical skills, as with Captain Coffey. Golfer Jack Nicklaus, skier Ingemar Stenmark, diver Sylvie Bernier, guitarist Pepe Romero, and cancer surgeon Bernie Siegel are among those who have used and praised the value of imagery in enhancing performance.

Just as physical effort and practice create pathways of association between our bodies and minds, mental pictures influence our physical capabilities by stimulating the same pathways. I did a review of psychological literature as a graduate student in 1971 that compared the effects of mental physical practice on physical performance. Out of 24 studies, only four concluded that physical practice was superior; one study actually found mental practice to be superior. What forcefully indicated the power of imagery was that in 19 out of the 24 studies, mental and physical practice were found to be equally important.

Imagery is first and foremost a language. It is the forgotten language of our youth. In *The Mature Mind*, H.A. Overstreet says, "The arrested development of the imagination is, perhaps, the most common tragedy of our human existence." The power of the imagination has been the subject of much research in recent years. Unfortunately, the research is usually expressed in language that's difficult for the layman to understand. In an article entitled "Brain Structures Participating in Mental Simulation of Motor Behavior: A Neuropsychological Interpretation," in the journal *Acta Psychologica*, Jean Decety, of the Institut de la Santé et de la Recherche Médicale in Brun, France, and David Ingvar, of University Hospital in Lund, Sweden, summarized the literature investigating the use of imagery in sports psychology and neurophysiology as follows:

This paper reviews findings from cognitive and sport psychology, as well as from neurophysiology, concerning mental simulation of movement. A neuropsycholgical hypothesis is advanced to explain why mental practice can improve motor skill learning. Mental practice activates certain brain structures selectively as shown by measurement of regional cerebral blood flow. It appears likely that this activation improves the subsequent control of execution of movements. It is pointed out that the study of simulation of movement may not only be of value for sport training but also have importance in the rehabilitation of patients with motor disturbances following lesions of the central nervous system.

In plain, everyday English it seems apparent that mental imagery is a powerful skill that can improve not only performance, but also personal health. And it can be applied to almost any ordinary situation. When we are relaxed (and we can get that way through the relaxation exercise described in the chapter on Energy Management), we are more open to images. But we are ahead of ourselves. Let's start with a general discussion of the concept of imagery, to help us understand how and why it works at a personal level.

Imagery: an introduction

Imagine for a moment that you are sitting in a chair, and I put you under hypnosis. While you're hypnotized, I take an everyday wristwatch, shake it a little in front of you, and say, "This is a live snake." Then I throw it in your lap. What do you do? Well, if you're like most people, you jump— unless you're extremely fond of snakes, in which case you gently stroke the snake (please remember, always with the scales). Why are you reacting this way? It's not a snake, it's a wristwatch.

Well, in hypnosis, the conscious mind is put to sleep. The message goes directly to the subconscious mind, which does not distinguish between a real or an imaginary experience. Stop and think about that for a moment. Our subconscious mind, the sum total of all our human experiences to this point in our lives, doesn't distinguish between those things we imagine and those things we actually do. That is why imagery works.

Hypnosis is not necessary for imagery to function; I mention it here only to make the point that the subconscious mind treats images as real. We have many experiences in our subconscious mind that we have imagined but have never undergone, and these are treated as real. Imagine, for example, that you're home late at night during a thunderstorm, and you don't feel comfortable alone in the house. You decide to take a shower before you go to bed. As you walk into the bathroom, does Alfred Hitchcock's *Psycho* come to mind? None of us was murdered in *Psycho,* and yet for some of us the image of the shower scene in that movie is so strong that it will keep us out of the shower on lonely, spooky nights. Others of us who manage to summon the courage to get into the shower will pull back the curtain partway through to make sure we're safe. All of this, in spite of the fact that we know, intellectually at least, that there's really nobody else in the house. It doesn't matter, does it? If we imagine that we are in danger, we experience the same inner climate as if we were.

At the turn of the century Émile Coué said, "When the imagination and the willpower are in conflict, are antagonistic, it is always the imagination that wins, without any exception." If we want something badly, we can muster all our willpower, but if we can't imagine it happening because of present circumstances, lack of self-esteem, the person whom we're married to, or the company we're working for, no matter how much we want it, it's never going to happen. The imagination is more powerful than willpower.

The subconscious mind always tries to create reality from the images and thoughts presented to it. If I say to you, "please don't imagine a blue elephant with pink running shoes", initially you imagine it, then the conscious mind quickly wipes it out. This hypersuggestibility is the main reason I insist on positive self-talk and positive images. Anyone trying to maintain a mental readiness for high performance cannot afford to feed on negative subconscious fodder.

Of course, you can't help but create an image when I suggest a blue elephant with pink running shoes. Most of you produced an image of that elephant. Whether we're cooking something on a stove, designing an ad campaign, or about to hit a golf ball, we begin with an image in our minds. Imagery is a line of communication with our inner world. It's a vital tool for finding inner calm, for planning, for working smarter, for self-healing, for improving performance, and it's key to developing a personal vision.

But the concept of imagery is more complex than seeing pictures. Some people experience a visual component of their imagery; others do not. World figure-skating champion Brian Orser, for example, did not have pictures in his imagery, but he heard his imagined performance and he felt it. Imagery means using as many of the senses as possible in order to present a complete multisensory "image" to the subconscious mind. This, in part, explains one of the differences between imagery and fantasy. Imagery brings to bear all that you would experience in reality at any given moment to the formation of that image. Fantasy, on the other hand, is flighty and distant. If I am not capable of doing something, I can't possibly generate the feelings, sounds, and sensations required to create a complete image.

Studies on basketball, for example, show that people who have never shot a basketball are unlikely to be able to imagine themselves doing so. But once they have tried a few shots, they are then able to create an image with greater ease because they know what it feels like. I have found that elite athletes can visualize only things that they can do or are close to being able to do. Only when they get close to being able to perfect a skill can they generate the feelings, emotions, and sounds necessary to complete the image of that skill.

Let's stop here and go through a miniature imagery exercise. After all, this book is meant to be an experience, not an intellectual exercise. As you read the following script, pause after each sentence and imagine (however you do it), the images I suggest. Gives yourself permission to try this, suspending judgment. You may wish to record this exercise on audiotape, pausing five to six seconds where the script uses an ellipsis (...) to indicate a time gap to reflect; then try to create the imagery at the audio cue of your own voice.

Sit in a relaxed position and imagine that you are in a kitchen. Perhaps your kitchen...(close your eyes now and imagine that). Listen for any sounds you might hear in this place...See the colors that you would see in this room...Smell the smells of the kitchen...Walk slowly over to the refrigerator and pull the door handle. Feel its resistance...The cold air wafts out as you open the door...The light is on in the fridge...Go to that place in the fridge where you might keep fruit...Reach in and take out a big yellow lemon...Feel the weight of the lemon in your hand, its texture...the coolness of its skin...Now close the door and walk over to where you might cut up fruit—a cutting board or a counter—and put the lemon on the cutting surface...Pick up the knife...Feel its weight and balance in your hand...Now cut the lemon in half, see the beads of juice on the knife blade, smell the faint smell of the lemon...Pick up half of that lemon and bring it to your nose and smell that clean, sharp scent...Put the lemon back down on the cutting board and cut the lemon into quarters...Pick up a quarter of the lemon and feel how you hold it in your fingertips...and bring it to your mouth and touch it to your lips, feeling how cool it is...And now take a giant bite into that lemon, feel the juice as it squirts in the back of your throat and tongue...Put the lemon back on the cutting board and come back into the room where you are reading this book.

Reflecting on this imagery exercise, circle the number that relates to your experience:

	NOT AT ALL						VERY CLEARLY			
1. Could you smell the lemon?	1	2	3	4	5	6	7	8	9	10
2. Could you "feel" the lemon, door handle, etc.?	1	2	3	4	5	6	7	8	9	10
3. Could you taste the lemon?	1	2	3	4	5	6	7	8	9	10
4. Could you hear sounds?	1	2	3	4	5	6	7	8	9	10
5. Did you have clear pictures?	1	2	3	4	5	6	7	8	9	10
6. Could you see colors?	1	2	3	4	5	6	7	8	9	10
7. Could you sense your body moving?	1	2	3	4	5	6	7	8	9	10
8. Other _____	1	2	3	4	5	6	7	8	9	10

What did you notice about how your imagination communicates? Could you smell the lemon? Some people get a strong sense of smell when they visualize, for others, it's faint. Because our imagery is a reflection of how we experience the world, it is likely that there is a high correlation between how conscious we are of smell in the external world and how strongly that sense figures in our imagery. And if your sense of smell is strong, it may also be that your memories are coded through smell.

This is true of all the other sensations included in the observation sheet. Each of us has our own coding system to which we are predisposed, and all of the possible sensations combine in varying degrees of prominence for each of us. Let me prompt you with some questions that will assist you in assessing how your own imagery functions and communicates. Could you feel the handle of the door when you wrapped your hand around it in your imagination? Could you feel the weight of the lemon and the texture of its skin? Each of these images involves touch, yet each creates a slightly different sensation. How tuned in are you to touch?

Could you feel yourself moving across the floor? Could you feel the movements of your body? From an athletic perspective, it is important, particularly when rehearsing a physical skill, to get the feeling of the movement. Most athletes have a strong kinesthetic component to their imagery; they sense the muscular effort in every movement of their body. I have often heard skaters talk about their imagery as if they are moving in their mind. They'll say, "I just landed a jump." They may be in the car or in class—it doesn't matter—they are capable of experiencing the kinesthetic sensation of landing a jump in their mind. This is spontaneous imagery. It is going on all the time. You, too, may sometimes get this kind of sensation, which may or may not seem strange to you, and wonder why. It isn't hard to find the answer. Look to your imagery. We're not used to paying attention in a conscious way to what we imagine, but remember: so much of what we have been talking about is based on developing our awareness of what is going on inside. The same is true for our self-talk, the stream of thoughts that continuously flow through our mind. Once we start to pay attention, we begin to observe a rich, but sometimes unsettling, flow of thoughts and images.

Did you hear any sounds? I didn't introduce noises, but you may have heard some familiar sounds from your kitchen—a radio in the background, the sound the refrigerator door made when it opened and closed. What happened when you bit into the lemon? It's fun to watch the facial maneuvers of people doing this part of the exercise. It is quite common for people to pucker, grimace, laugh, and smack their lips. Many people report more saliva in their mouth or a slight tensing at the back of their jaw. This is a good example of the power of imagery to create a physical reality within the body, particularly since the release of saliva is considered to be an involuntary response.

Finally, what did you see? Are you part of the majority who get a visual image, or were the pictures elusive? Were you in your body looking out at your kitchen, or were you outside of your body watching yourself perform? We don't know if there is any significance to first-party as opposed to third-party imagery, but it is informative to note which you use. Did you see color? Notice your own style of visualizing. If you don't pick up a lot of visual detail in your imagery, it may be that you don't pay much attention to visual detail in life. You may cue your behavior to things that aren't visual. Whatever way you visualize is your unique style. Learning to expand your imagery vocabulary and diversify the places you use it is one of the keys to moving to high performance. And, as with most things within our power, there is always room for improvement. Imagery is a skill, and like other skills, it improves dramatically when we use it.

Elite performers take imagery very seriously. In 1984 Sylvie Bernier won the gold medal in diving at the Los Angeles Olympics. Here's how she described her imagery sessions:

> I did my dives in my head all the time. At night, before going to sleep, I always did my dives. Ten dives. I started with a front dive, the first one that I actually had to do at the Olympics, and I did everything as if I was actually there. I saw myself on the board in the same bathing suit. Everything was the same. I saw myself in the pool at the Olympics doing my dives. If the dive was wrong, I went back and started over again. It takes a good hour to do perfect imagery of all my dives, but for me it was better than a workout. Sometimes I would take the weekend off and do imagery five times a day.

I felt like I was on the board and I did each dive so many times in my mind.

Because imagery is the language of our imagination, we are unlimited in how we use it. We can zoom in, or we can use a wide-angle lens. We can see it first-party, as if we were looking through our eyes at that moment, or we can see it third-party, as if we were watching ourselves on television. Laurie Graham, winner of five World Cup ski races, describes first-party imagery this way: "I don't watch myself. I visualize the race as if I'm running it. The course is coming at me."

Decathlete Michael Smith initially did his imagery much as Laurie Graham did, using first-party imagery, but he eventually moved to third-party imagery, where he mentally sees himself from outside. He attributes the change partially to television; he has watched himself so frequently on TV and video that he now has a clear picture of how he looks when he's performing. However, when he is running through third-party imagery, although he sees himself from the outside, he still feels all that he is doing and he hears the accompanying sounds. It's as if he is in his body, but his perspective is third-party. This is the kinesthetic component of his imagery.

Of course, athletes aren't the only ones to effectively use imagery. Bob works in sales. When a client calls, he creates within himself an image that the client is not satisfied with his current supplier. He uses that image to boost his confidence level to complete the sale. We all have our favorite ways to use imagery. Perhaps we are hosting a dinner party and we visualize how we want the table to look; then we work backward to make that happen. But why not use it in other ways, as well? The carpenter uses imagery when designing cabinets or figuring out where to hang a door, but what about using it to build his confidence or work out a problem with one of his children? Why limit the use of such a valuable and powerful tool?

The use of imagery is pervasive in our consumer society. Consider the way most products are sold. Advertisers want to create an image in your mind. Picture yourself, the radio commercial says, driving up your driveway in a brand-new General Motors product. See it parked in front of your house. If you can buy into that image, there's a likelihood that you will eventually buy the product. Imagery is so powerful that it is virtually the only mode of advertising.

It's not difficult to use imagery to improve your performance, but it does take time and it does take creativity, ambition, drive, and willpower. It takes a lot of willpower, for example, after a sales call that hasn't gone well, to stop, imagine that call, draw the lessons from it, and replay how you would like to do it another time. It takes willpower to choose to run the improved performance image, as opposed to dwelling on the negative image of what went wrong. You will find that you improve quickly when you consciously use imagery in your day-to-day experiences.

Special effects

Let's look at some of the ways that you can create and individualize imagery to fit the way you best receive information.

Greatest hits

This refers to the art of locating emotions from past successful experiences. The subconscious mind is a memory bank of feelings and images from your past triumphs, your own mental Hall of Fame. Elite athletes tap into this memory bank to prepare for a competition by "rewinding" to those previously experienced feelings and then "fast-forwarding" to the upcoming challenge. Maybe you gave a brilliant speech at a wedding once; you can get in touch with how you felt during and after that performance, then fast-forward to an important speech you have to give to the Home and School Association tonight. One of the wonderful things about imagery is that you can "cheat." You can steal from the past and project the feelings and images of success onto the future.

Zoom, volume, and color adjustments

You can zoom in and out. You can turn the volume up and down. You can remove the color. You can add to the color. You can gradually shrink and blur images to diminish their importance to you. There are thousands of possibilities for fine-tuning your internal images, particularly to let go of mental obstacles in your way. Focus on something that's really bothering you and imagine it dwindling to the size of a piece of paper, then crumple that paper, put it inside a black box, and put that black box behind you. You can reduce an object until it is tiny, blow it into a helium balloon, and imagine the balloon drifting way until it disappears into the sky. You can gradually turn the volume down on self-talk that is negative and critical. I'm sure that you can think of a multitude of other adjustments.

Use of metaphors and symbols

The balloon, the black box, the crumpled paper—all of these images are examples of metaphors or symbols. When metaphors are included in your imagery, they speak to you at the mind, body, and feeling level. Many people perform their imagery in metaphoric or symbolic ways. In his golf column, Jack Nicklaus describes using an automobile pulling away from a stop sign as an image to control the speed of his back swing. It's a perfect metaphor that saves him thousands of words. The automobile starts slowly and gradually picks up speed—exactly what the golfer wants to do with his back swing.

Here's a parable that I often refer to when I am trying to let go of things that I have no control over. In Southeast Asia, there is a tribe that captures monkeys by filling a cage with bananas and leaving it out in the open. A monkey comes down from the trees, investigates the cage, and finds a hole just big enough to push its paw through. It reaches in and grabs a banana, but it cannot pull its paw back out of the cage because the banana, which it is holding, is too large. Now the natives come out from behind their camouflaged hiding place, pick the monkey up, and put it in the cage. The monkey was caught because it had such a desire for the banana that it wouldn't let go of it.

The image of the monkey's hand caught in the cage with the banana is a metaphor for those things we hang on to that, once released, would make us freer—the need to ensure that the toilet-paper roll always feeds over the top, the need to be perfect, the need to change other people. I was once told that there are three effective ways to change another person: long-term psychotherapy, a deep religious experience, or a frontal lobotomy. That's not to say that people don't change. People can change, but change is an inside job, and when we have worked with some people for five or six years, or lived with them for ten, and we're still constantly trying to change them, we are trapped by senseless striving. We are stuck in a country-and-western song!

A good story shows us symbolically what we are doing and changes our perception—in the case of the monkey story, allowing me to let go of something. You can use metaphors to communicate with yourself. Relating things metaphorically distances us from them, yet we can call up those images to get a clear message when, for example, we're trying to let go of something, find a new perspective, or be more patient.

In a recent workshop I challenged the participants to come up with a metaphoric image that they might use to stop negative, critical inner dialogue. One man came up with the following: "When self-talk is endlessly repeating a negative message, I get an image of a record that is stuck, going around and around, playing the same message. I imagine that I take the needle, drag it across the record, and turn the record over. On the other side is the positive message that I want to hear. I choose to turn the record over and play that message." This is an excellent example of the use of metaphor in imagery. If we just let an image come to us of what a situation or issue feels like, the image often becomes a personal metaphor that we can use to transcend mental obstacles. It is true, isn't it, that negative self-talk sometimes is like a record that's stuck? We'll talk more about metaphors and symbols when we discuss uses of imagery in the section on letting go of inappropriate thoughts and feelings.

Scenario performing

Groucho Marx once stood up at a cocktail party and sang a beautiful aria. Someone said to him afterward, "I didn't know you could sing opera." Marx replied, "I can't. I was imitating Caruso." You don't always have to be yourself in imagery. Sometimes you can ask yourself the question "How would my hero or heroine handle this?" You imagine him or her acting out the situation.

Scenario performing is also excellent for problem solving. It's a great way to move off a plateau when we don't have any idea about a solution or can't see ourselves carrying the solution out. When you imagine, for example, someone else resolving a conflict at work, you see all kinds of options that you might not have considered. You see how this person might use humor, for instance, and how that approach might be different from the one you would take. An office manager told me she had to do an unpleasant performance appraisal with one of her employees, with whom she had had a long-term conflict. She imagined how someone else in the office would handle the difficulty. She saw the humor that the other person would use. She saw the creative way that the person would deal with the difficult and negative bits of feedback that that employee needed to receive.

All sorts of humor is associated with scenario performing, as one golfer found out: he was playing brilliantly in a tournament, imagining all the time that he was Arnold Palmer.

The trouble was the opponent who beat him was imagining he was Jack Nicklaus.

Problems in the projection room

Sometimes when you try to imagine something there is a gap in the film, or the picture gets hazy or turns upside down. This is often an indication that you do not have a clear idea of how to proceed at that moment, so you may want to make sure you have enough information. At other times, the difficulty in seeing a complete picture is an indication that you are trying to do something that you just don't feel comfortable doing at that moment. Using the example of a performance appraisal, you may see the beginning and end of the interview, but in the middle, when you should be thinking of the things you want to tell the employee, your picture becomes fuzzy, or white lines are running through it. You may not have a clear idea of how to proceed at that moment with this person, given your history with that person and the tension that exists between you. This, as we mentioned in the scenario-performing section, is a great opportunity to imagine somebody else handling the situation. You will find, once you do that, that your picture clears up, the gap in the film is replaced by this person performing the activity, and gradually, as I mentioned earlier, you will replace that person with yourself in your imagery.

Sometimes during your imagery you will get a sudden flash picture that you're falling, or making a terrible mistake. This is not an indication that you are going to fall or make a mistake; sometimes it's your subconscious telling you to pay attention to a particular item or issue. Go back and replay that item. Other times it's a message to make sure that you stick to your strategy and pay attention to what you're doing.

Early in the morning one day, just as it was beginning to get light, I was running on a roadway that was unfamiliar. I suddenly got an image that I rolled over on my ankle and sprained it. I used to think that these images were premonitions, that I had to stop running and carefully walk home. I now realize that often when I get images I don't expect, it's the intuitive side of my brain telling me to pay attention. In this instance, "Pay attention! Watch where you're putting your feet!" I looked down and saw that the road was full of potholes. I realized that I was daydreaming (I prefer to call it "imagery") and wasn't paying attention to what I was doing. Often, these images are a message that we should pay attention to the speech, or the job interview, or whatever we were rehearsing at that moment.

Making your imagery work for you

Here are four key steps to ensure that your imagery works for you:

Clarify your intention
Tell yourself clearly why you are about to do an imagery exercise. Your intention provides the basic "thoughtware," the direction-setting mechanism for your practice. The clearer your intention, the better the quality of your result.

Relax
Imagery is most effective when you know what you want and are relaxed. Your brain switches from an active mode to a more receptive mode. Bringing down your arousal level and going into a deeply relaxed state is a key to successful imagery. Here are a few guidelines to help you relax deeply. With practice you can be ready within 30 seconds:

- Focus gently on your breathing; pay quiet attention to the inflow of air and the exhalation of each breath. Do not try to do your breathing.
- Clear your mind. Turn down your observer switch. Simply watch your thoughts come and go like passing clouds in the sky.

- Use a specific relaxation technique. Try progressive relaxation: tighten all your muscles, count from 10 to one staying tense, then release all the tension at the count of one.
- Use verbal cues, such as "relax," or "going down, down, down." Or use picture cues such as seeing a quiet relaxing environment.

Do your imagery work

Put your own program together, using the following scenarios:

- "Getting there" images. Imagine yourself performing beautifully, doing things exactly the way you want them done. Feel the smooth rhythmical flow.
- Results images. Be, see, and feel the impact of having accomplished your intention. Experience the end of your journey, the completion of the project, the end of the event.

Reconnect

Come back from your inner workout feeling calmer, refreshed, and focused on the task at hand. Connect your feelings and your imagery with what you have to do or with how you want to feel.

Timing and detail in imagery

It's important to talk about timing when we talk about imagery. If imagery is, as we have suggested, an actual rehearsal as far as the body is concerned, then it's important that the timing be the same as it would be in real life. Jean-Claude Killy, the French skier, used to say that he could time his imagery and always be within one second of his real race time.

If you rehearse something and find that the rehearsal is twice as fast as the actual performance, then you should add some detail to your imagery. In sport, where timing is critical, I often time an athlete's imagery prior to an event. Without revealing the time, I compare it with the time I know the athlete wants to perform in, then I encourage him or her to either slow down or speed up the imagery accordingly. I was working with figure skater Elvis Stojko at the World Figure Skating Championships in Munich in 1990, when he said, "You know, whenever I do my quadruple jump in my imagery, I feel rushed. When I image it there's a white flash." He added more detail to his imagery, which slowed the playing out of the imagery, and allowed the jump to come out of him. He subsequently landed a quad-double combination, the first ever performed in competition.

Uses and applications

The following are some suggested ways to use imagery. This is by no means a complete list, but rather some examples so you can see how others have proceeded:

Mental rehearsal

We can use imagery to mentally rehearse almost anything, to get in touch with the event and how it will feel. It's essential that the mental rehearsal involve the feelings, the sensations, and the experiences that will actually occur. This, for example, is not mental rehearsal: "I float in to the budget committee meeting. I am blindingly brilliant. The budget committee offers me twice as much money as I was asking for. I float out of the meeting."

That...is fantasy. Imagery is feeling the increase in heart rate and the sweaty palms as you stand before the budget committee. It is feeling, hearing, and sensing the impact that tough questions will have on you. It is also seeing yourself respond to those questions, lowering your arousal level, making eye contact with every member in the room. It is the colors, the personalities, the atmosphere—all in vivid detail.

When I ask athletes prior to a performance how they feel, invariably I get the same answer: "Awful. My heart's pounding. I'm anxious. I just want to get this over with." When I ask them, "Are you surprised by this?" They almost always say, "No, I'm not surprised. When I did my imagery I knew I was going to feel like this. So it's normal to feel like this. It's okay to feel like this because, in my imagery, although I felt like this I performed very well. I'm not surprised by the way I feel."

As I go into a job interview, it's no surprise that my heart rate is up and my palms are sweating. I expected that in my imagery. My imagery has also made it clear that this is a sign that I am ready. In my imagery I have dealt extremely well with the situation and mentally rehearsed the successful completion of the job interview. I do the same with the putt under pressure on the golf course, the toast to the bride at the wedding, the difficult problem I'm having with my children. As you can well imagine, there are as many uses of mental rehearsal as there are situations that exist for us to deal with.

Letting go of irrelevant thoughts, feelings, and distractions
Imagery is effective in allowing us to let go of things that we don't have to attend to anymore, that we shouldn't be attending to at this moment, or that are dramatically interfering with our concentration. The technique of "releasing" is well described by Patricia Carrington in her book of the same name. Again, your imagination is the only limitation on the number of ways to let go of things. I can imagine an object, thought, or person that is currently interfering with my effectiveness. I can imagine the sensation of that object, thought, or person flowing down my arm. I can squeeze my arm tightly and sense what it feels like to uselessly hang on to something, sense the tightness and discomfort in my hand. Then I can say, "Let it go," and open my hand and experience how good it feels to release that object, thought, or person. The ball image discussed earlier that the coun-

selors of abused women and children employed to disidentify is another excellent example of using imagery to let go; another is the balloon that floats away into the distance, taking worry with it.

Sometimes we don't want to release something; we want to put it aside and deal with it later. "Parking," which Linda Thom mentioned in her distraction plan, is the skill that allows us to put things aside temporarily to focus on the matter at hand. If I'm trying to write a report but the work load that is awaiting me constantly comes into my mind, I stop and I imagine the work load. I imagine it, I drive it over, and I park it as if it were a car. Then I come back and focus on the task at hand. Obviously I have to deal with that work load eventually, but right now I just park it. That may allow me 10, 15, even 20 minutes of undisturbed concentration. I may have to use the parking technique or another technique when the work load comes to mind again. Maybe the next time I'll put it in my black box and imagine that I pick up my black box, turn my body around, and put it behind me. Here I am not just using imagery; I'm using my body, as well, to physically put the work load behind me.

Ottawa sports psychologist Terry Orlick describes a technique that the people of Papua, New Guinea, call "treeing." They hang a particular "disturbance" up in a tree for a while and go back and get it later when they have time to deal with it. Often, when they go back to get the problem, they find out that it's disappeared or isn't of concern anymore, or that it's shrunk in size. Others imagine a problem swishing down the drain or, more dramatically, flushing down the toilet. I'm sure that you can come up with images and metaphors that you can use to let go of things you no longer wish to concern yourself with, or things you wish to put aside so that you can concentrate on what you must do at the moment.

Here's a story that I use to let go of things when they hang on too long and interfere with what I am trying to do at the moment. Centuries ago two monks—one young and one old—were out walking, when they came to a stream. On one side of the stream was a young woman who had fallen from her horse and badly sprained her ankle. On the other side of the stream was her horse. She said to the younger of the two monks, "Would you be so kind as to pick me up, carry me across the stream, and put me on my horse? I live but a few moments from here and will be safe." And the young monk said, with great sadness and in total truth, "Alas, I cannot, for I have taken a vow of chastity. I may never touch a woman." And he walked across the stream regretfully. The old monk, without saying a word, bent down, picked the young women up, and carried her across the water, where he put her on her horse and sent the horse on its way. The monks walked all day in total silence. Finally, as evening fell, the young monk could contain himself no longer. He turned to the old monk and said, "I cannot believe you picked that woman up." "Ah," said the old monk, "I put her down eight hours ago...but you, you are still carrying her."

Relaxation and energizing

There are numerous ways of using imagery to relax. Perhaps after doing the lemon exercise you felt relaxed when you finished, despite the unpleasantness of mentally biting into a lemon. Imagery creates a relaxed state within us by going in at the mind, body, and feeling level. A CEO told me that in important meetings he uses a technique he learned as a baseball player years ago. As a shortstop he would constantly check his hands to make sure they were loose and relaxed so that he could receive the ball gently and make the throw to first base. The technique really worked in the crucial late innings. Now he uses his "soft-hands" image when he goes into meetings in which he has to be open and receptive. He sees himself receiving and reacting with smoothness and fluidity through all that he faces.

Images are individual. A beach may be a relaxing image for you, but it may not be for a colleague. Someone told me that when he found himself getting anxious and nervous in performance appraisals, he simply put his hand under the table and imagined warm sand running through his fingers. That image allowed him to lower his arousal level and get out what he was capable of doing. That was his moment-to-moment relaxation image. What would you use?

We all have images of our favorite place in nature that we can use to become more relaxed in critical moments. If you become aware that your energy level is too high before a high-pressure presentation, you might imagine that you're on a beach, or that sand is running through your fingers; or that you're floating on a cloud, canoeing at your cottage, or meditating by a beautiful waterfall. Use your own relaxation images. If, on the other hand, you have made this presentation many times before, with the result that your energy level is too low and your mind is wandering, you can use imagery to energize. You can get in touch with the way you want to feel at the end of the talk and run some images that are powerful and motivating. Combining these with the skill of parking that we just talked about, you can, for example, park feelings of fatigue and immerse yourself in the "read and react" mode, seeing yourself reading and reacting to the challenges of your immediate environment and staying in touch with how important the presentation is to you.

If you're sitting at your desk at the middle of the day, feeling flat and unenergized, yet you have lots of work to do, running an image of finishing your day without the work done and going home knowing that you'll have that pile of work waiting for you tomorrow may be enough to motivate you to get at the task at hand. That imagery may sound negative at first, but it's a good way to use your feelings to mobilize your resources to move forward.

Problem solving

"Some people see things as they are and ask, 'Why?' Others see them as they ought to be and ask, 'Why not?'" said Robert Kennedy. Albert Einstein said, "To raise new questions, new possibilities, to regard old problems from a new angle, requires creative imagination and marks real advance in science." Both Kennedy's and Einstein's aphorisms relate to our discussion of imagery. Kennedy's allusion to "seeing things" and Einstein's to a new "angle" and "creative imagination" indicate that they both viewed imagery as a part of problem solving. Images and metaphors that help us to step back and gain perspective can create order out of chaos.

During meetings where conflicts arise, a businessman I know physically pushes his chair slightly back from the table. In his mind's eye, he stands back from the table, and from that perspective he truly sees what is going on. He sees the group dynamics and the bottlenecks. From that distance, he can get an emotionally removed view and recognize patterns that he could not see up close.

My wife, Sandra Stark, once led a group of architects through a relaxation and imagery session to help them "see" how to solve tricky design problems. She guided them through the finished structure that they were trying to design, and when they went back to their brainstorming session, they had four times as many ideas as they had before the guided imagery tour. They got in touch with the creative side of their brains, the side that sees in pictures and in wholes, but has no words.

To see with a new perspective, sometimes we have to choose to take that perspective. In our imagination we can use any vantage point. We can take the role of "the other" to see the impact of our plans and strategy on those around us.

What is the impact of this information? With whom am I communicating? Am I communicating in a style that might rile the other person? By taking the other person's perspective, by literally getting into his shoes and imagining that I am receiving the message that I am giving, I can collect all kinds of information that I need to properly package my presentation and get the desired outcome.

Adjusting to new environments

If I know, for example, that I have an important interview two weeks from now in the boardroom of company ABC, I make every attempt to see that room before the meeting so that I can imagine my mental rehearsals for the meeting in that environment for the next two weeks. Through mental rehearsal and imagery, I adapt and begin to feel comfortable in that room.

Athletes, of course, do this all the time. They can't possibly train physically at the Olympic site five months before the games, but mentally they can train there once they know the lay of the land. They can begin, in their imagination, to be there every day, and thus be familiar and comfortable with the environment when they arrive. Diver Sylvie Bernier landed in the water in Montreal during training, but she dove mentally in Los Angeles every day.

Motivation

I had just finished addressing 450 doctors at a medical convention, when Peter Welsh, an orthopedic surgeon and a former steeplechase runner for New Zealand, got up to thank me. "You know, sports psychologists have proven only two things," he said. "One is that 95 percent of runners, in order to stay motivated during running, engage in sexual imagery. But," he said, delivering the punchline, "only 5 percent of people, while engaged in sex, imagine running." Well, I'm not sure of Peter's statistics, but I am sure that imagery is a potent skill for motivation.

From the sales manager who imagines her product on the store shelf before making a sales call, then "sees" the successful sale and does what she has to do to make that happen, to the athlete who imagines himself winning the gold medal, many people motivate themselves through visions of what is possible. Many put slogans of their visions up on a wall to develop a powerful image (they act as affirmations). In the next chapter we will deal in more detail with motivation and imagery. I just want to make the point here that images motivate people to buy things all the time, and they can motivate us, if we develop a strong personal image, to accomplish what we wish to accomplish and be the way we want to be.

Health

In 1988 I received a phone call from Dr. Dennis Gersten, a physician in San Diego who uses imagery in his treatment of patients. Dennis had decided that it was time for a journal on imagery, and had contacted me and a variety of other people who were using imagery in the areas of performance and health, such as Bernie Siegel, Carl Simonton, Naomi Remen, Jeanne Achterberg, and others. I was thrilled to be associated with such a renowned group of professionals.

Dennis brought this group together to act as a resource for a journal called *Atlantis, The Imagery Newsletter.* The majority of its articles deal with healing for patients and healthcare professionals. Guiding images and approaches are presented in each article, many of them developed by patients harnessing their inner resources to deal with their illnesses or bolstering themselves for greulling treatment programs. These range from attack and transformational images, to healing and psychological symbols; from imagining what is going on in their bodies and how to heal it, to getting in touch with symbols of wellness and, if you will, their own inner adviser.

A woman in my workshop told me she had a lot of trouble with the "isolate," "annihilate," "destroy," and "surround" war terminology frequently used in cancer treatment. She had to find more peaceful images, because she didn't want to imagine a war going on inside her body. She uses the image of a woman in long, flowing, white robes, gently cleansing all the sections of her body that need cleansing. The important thing is to find the image that you are comfortable with, the image that works for you.

Engaging in imagery and other self-help practices allows people who are seeking to attain better health take control of and assume responsibility for themselves. That in itself is a valuable asset for every person trying to move toward optimal health. But the evidence also points to a dramatic impact on human physiology, as well. Healing imagery appears, according to some research studies, to increase the body's defence systems, rallying the troops to assist in dealing with illness. Take a look back at cancer patient Debby Rudack's discussion of her imagery in Chapter Two.

The ways we can use imagery to move to a more healthy state are varied. The quest might involve uncovering and dealing with things from our past that are eating away at us unconsciously. Because we have not paid attention to them, they have begun to harm us physiologically, in order to jolt us into thinking about what is happening in our lives. It might mean deciding how we want to look or the kind of shape, in terms of personal health and well-being, we see ourselves in 10 years from now.

When we have an image of how we want to be, it is much easier to harness our resources to move toward that image. It is not my intention to go into more detail here on the role of imagery in health and personal well-being. There are numerous excellent books available on the subject by Bernie Siegel, Joan Borysenko, Carl Simonton, and many others. But if you are currently dealing with an illness in your life, I would strongly suggest that you look into the uses of imagery in enhancing your inner resources.

Final tips on imagery work

You've got to believe

Imagery is a powerful tool, but you have to choose to believe it can work for you. Without belief, it will be difficult to create the emotions and sensations that enhance imagery.

Go for the full treatment

Work with all the senses and heighten the intensity, the color, the movement, and the feelings—the more vivid the better. Be playful with your images. Let loose. Let them grow and expand, and above all, be creative.

Take it seriously
Take the time to do it properly and you will get quality results. Jack Nicklaus says, "I never hit a golf ball—not once, not in practice, not in competition—without first getting a clear image of the flight of the ball and seeing it land up high on the green." For Nicklaus, imagery is a part of every single stroke he makes. It is essential to the way he approaches everything that he does in a round of golf.

Keep written notes
Learn from your experiences. Don't let images that work for you slip away. Increase your visual vocabulary. Often we drift away from things that work for us because we just plain forget that we used to use them.

Just do it, do it, and do it
Do 30-second, two-minute, or more detailed rehearsals time after time, and stick with it. Imagery is a skill that improves significantly with use. Studies with elite athletes show that almost no one starts out with perfect, clear imagery, but with practice it improves dramatically.

CHAPTER NINE

Visioneering

The reasonable man adapts himself to the world. The unreasonable one persists in trying to adapt the world to himself. Therefore all progress depends on the unreasonable man.
—George Bernard Shaw.

Winning is not "normal." The Mother Teresas, the Gandhis, the Martin Luther Kings are not normal. Yet ordinary people do extraordinary things all the time. "Dream big dreams," said a professor of mine, "for only big dreams have the power to excite the magic in people's minds." This is the most important chapter in the book and thus the hardest to write. Personal vision is an integral part of every great success, but there are no formulas for developing your own vision. This chapter is thus a smorgasbord of quotes and ideas, but I hope it will present some guidelines.

The trick is to say yes to life. Arriving at a life vision can appear to be a complex process; however, in the end it's relatively simple.

What is vision?

More people are limited by the size of their imagination and dreams than by any other single reality. I have worked with some extraordinary performers, all of whom were ordinary people. Some of them were athletic performers, some were cancer patients, some were corporate executives, but they all had a vision. Some of these people developed a vision late in life; others always had one.

Years ago I attended a workshop given by Marcella Rolicki. Partway through the workshop, Marcie, a wonderfully warm and creative woman who had survived the loss of a husband and a couple of bouts with cancer, played a cassette recording of the poem "I'd Pick More Daisies." In a voice laden with emotion, barely audible and cracking with each phrase, an 82-year old woman read, "If I had to do it over again, I'd pick more daisies. I'd eat more ice cream. I'd walk more country roads." When the tape was finished Marcie turned to us and asked, "How did you feel about that?" We talked about how sad we were that this woman had not carried out her vision. Not until the twilight of her life had she recognized how misdirected she had been. Marcie shocked us. "It's all bullshit," she said. "The country roads are still there. They're still making ice cream. The flowers are still growing. Why the heck doesn't she get on with it?"

Our vision, according to John Kenneth Galbraith, helps us determine what is really relevant from what is merely acceptable. Without vision, we often find that we've been walking the wrong path for many years. Sometimes a giant wake-up call—the collapse of the company, cancer, the loss of a loved one—jolts us into reality. We see that we have not been following a personal vision of the kind of future we'd like to see. And it goes much deeper than goals and broader than wishes. Vision gets at your unique gift—the contribution that you can make or the talent that you have. Visioneering is vision building; it's about personal empowerment, taking over your own life and tailoring your activities to meet your own capacities.

High-level performers know the power of a dream. After her silver-medal performance at the 1988 winter Olympics, figure skater Elizabeth Manley was interviewed by ABC's Peggy Fleming. The first words out of Liz's mouth, seconds after she had performed her long program, were about her dream. "I have been dreaming of this night for years," she told Fleming.

Vision ignites. Vision is your power switch. Vision is the energy that helps you through the difficult points in life. A few years ago I was doing a workshop in Amsterdam. Rick Hansen, who went around the world in a wheelchair in two years, two months, and two days, raising millions of dollars for spinal-cord research, was with me. When I finished talking about vision and the importance of imagery, he said, "You know, that's very much how I thought of it. I didn't use those words, but I remember how much energy I got from my vision. One rainy, miserable night in North Korea, the organizers of the tour told me, 'We promised you would visit an orphanage tomorrow, so we will have to go out of our way.' It was such a distance that it added two days to an already too long trip. There wasn't one thing in those next two days of work that made me want to do it. There wasn't one thing in the activity itself that made it worthwhile. It was only by getting in touch with my vision that I was able to get through those difficult times and find the energy to pull myself through."

There is often little in our day-to-day life that motivates us. It is so difficult to be pushed and shoved, poked and cajoled by what we face each day and so much easier to be *pulled* by our vision. What would possess anyone to become a competitive swimmer? Is it the odds of making the Olympic team? Imagine sitting down and figuring out the odds of becoming an Olympic swimmer—no one would ever start swimming. Is it the hours? Do swimmers really enjoy getting up at five in the morning, diving into a swimming pool, working for two and a half hours, then doing the same thing again late in the afternoon? Perhaps it's the scenery, going by the same swimming-pool wall and lane marker, hour after hour, day after day. Intrinsically, there's little in the activity that excites and motivates potential Olympic swimmers. They are pulled through the water by their vision, by their clear mental image of the future.

Why vision?

The research of my colleague Bob Wiele has shown: 1. no one gets out alive; 2. few of us want to leave early; 3. this is it—this is not a dry run; 4. each of us possesses a unique gift or talent, or has a unique contribution to make; 5. most of us don't make a commitment to our own creativity or allow our personal vision to flourish. We have three selves in our lives: the one we were born with, the one we now have as a result of our life choices in the past, and the one we create in the future by our life choices now.

Abraham Maslow, the distinguished psychologist best known for his theory of the hierarchy of needs, initiated the first studies on the mental and emotional makeup of high performers. He said that there were only two questions to be answered: "What do I really want in life?" and "What do I need for happiness?" Maslow's advice was to be all you can in life. It's the best way to be happy. He found that the high performers he studied had strong personal visions. They made full use of their talents and capabilities. He believed that fulfillment never comes from following the crowd, but only in being faithful to your own yearning and talents.

Dr. Lawrence LeShan (author of *You Can Fight for Your Life*) has studied the psychological patterns that precede the onset of cancer. His research has spanned more than three decades. His conclusions are that 70 to 80 percent of adults who contract cancer have experienced a loss of hope at a deep psychological level before the onset of their disease. They have lost hope that they could ever live their lives in a meaningful, zestful way. They have lost their belief in their capacity to express their own special song in life, the interest that gave them great joy. This deep emotional giving-up is a factor in the weakening of the immune system.

Uncovering your vision

In his book of the same name, Joseph Campbell describes "the hero's journey" as a central life task for all adults. He identifies three major stages of the journey:

The departure: In this first stage, you leave the comfort of what's known to reflect on what's important. The push can come from a major life change or a growing feeling inside that you need to explore new horizons. The mid-life crisis is a good example. The departure may be psychological only. Things that once had meaning no longer seem important. But there is no clear idea of what is needed next.

The search: A period of great confusion, personal anguish, and upheaval, internally and often in the external world, as well. The search often takes months, sometimes several years. We all know people who have made major life changes to follow their dream. A failure to confront the deep messages and yearnings that surface during this phase will come back to haunt you for the rest of your days.

The return: You come back, but you come back changed. You may look the same, but profound shifts in your interior landscape have occurred. There is now a surge of inner purpose and resolution. The mental clouds have cleared, and the internal sun has begun to shine. Elite athletes and outstanding performers in other fields describe this internal shift as "the commitment to the commitment." Visions must be turned into action. The litmus test of a personal vision is in what you do, not in what you think. There is a total commitment to "go for it," whatever your unique "it" may be.

But how do you uncover your own vision? There aren't clear and precise steps that you can take, although many will tell you that there are. Vision is such a personal thing that it takes a while to develop it. It's best to come at it from different sides. For job hunters, *What Color Is Your Parachute?* and *The Three Boxes of Life and How to Get Out of Them* by Richards Bowles can help get you in touch with a personal dream.

But for those of you who are already entrenched in what you're doing, I have found that sometimes the best bet is to start with uncovering a personal purpose. Why have you chosen to do what you're doing? Sometimes we get out of touch with our original motivations. (We become like janitors who hate dirt. No dirt, no janitor!) No one chains you to your current situation. Write several paragraphs on the path you have chosen, and when you have finished, after every sentence ask yourself one of two questions, whichever fits better: "Why?" or "What is the purpose of this?"

I did this exercise with one of the professional golfers on the LPGA tour, who wrote paragraphs involving her life and her family. After every sentence she asked herself, "Why?" or "What is the purpose of this?" It took her two or three hours, but eventually she realized that she'd chosen golf because she liked the challenge and the excitement of testing herself against others in front of an audience and seeing constant improvement. Her vision then became her mental linage of the future.

What if I don't reach my vision?

What if I have a clear and compelling mental image of the future and I never get there? Does that mean I have a lousy vision? No, not at all. Look at the heights that your vision has pulled you to. In the Olympic Games there is only one gold medalist for every event. The other competitors, who, as children dreamed of the gold medal and as teenagers used that dream to fire their practices—are they all failures? No, they certainly aren't. They've risen to incredible levels by following their dreams.

A thirtysomething female sales manager, the top salesperson in the country for Philips Electronics, approached me at a workshop. She had just been set a new sales quota of $8 million. She was experiencing fear of failure, because she knew the more successful she was, the higher the quota would become. Her clear and compelling mental image of the future was of herself eventually running her own company. So we talked about seeing this year as an investment in inner development; we reframed it so that we weren't focusing strictly on her performance.

The big question was would the $8-million sales quota affect her vision? Would not meeting it result in a drop in self-esteem and confidence and, as a consequence, discourage her from fulfilling her vision? "No," she said, "I can focus on inner growth, confidence, self-esteem, and carrying out my strategy. What I lose in financial income will be more than compensated for by the investment in myself." As a result, she will be a lot closer to attaining her vision and she'll probably reach her goal. What if she sold $2 million in a recession economy and was still ranked number one? Would she have failed? Not at all. When you align yourself with your vision, when you think and act like a champion and a professional, all other things begin to align themselves with your goals. Stephen Leacock said that he was a great believer in luck—the harder he worked, the more of it he acquired.

Goal setting

The first step is to invent your own future—establish your vision. The next step is to set goals, make the commitment, and act. Obviously your goals should be in line with your vision. If your goals are not aligned with your vision, you will not have the motivation, desire, and commitment necessary to achieve them. Your goals are what you need to acquire, learn, or change, in order to reach your vision.

There are many people whose goals are not in line with their vision because they have never uncovered their vision and purpose in the first place. So they set monetary goals, all the while unaware that there isn't much reference to money or ownership in their vision. Dustin Hoffman was asked once why he had left the lucrative California film market to star onstage in New York for more than five years in *Death of a Salesman.* He said that he missed the audience, and the audience is a huge part of who he is as a professional actor. His goals were clearly in line with his personal vision. This also is evident in his selection of roles for movies. He has yet to be typecast. *Tootsie, Rainman,* and *Midnight Cowboy* all presented him with different challenges that allowed him to expand as the consummate professional actor.

I was working with 12 corporate executives who were planning to retire in the next three to five years. I asked them to describe their mental images of the future. I asked them, "In 10 years, assuming the world is a fair and just place, what will your world look like?" They all wrote quite similar scenarios. They all talked about traveling. They had done a lot of traveling for business, but they hadn't had the opportunity to explore the countries they had visited. They also talked about family and relationships and personal health and well-being.

When it came to goal setting, I started with traveling. I asked them where they would be, financially, 10 years from now, because that would have an impact on how much traveling they could do. Money was not going to be a problem for this group. Given so much return on X amount of money, they could figure out, almost to the cent, where their finances would be 10 years hence.

Then I moved to the area of health, which, incidentally, had ranked as their number-one priority, the most important thing they wished to have 10 years down the road. I asked them, "Where will your blood pressure be 10 years from now?" "What a stupid bloody question!" a gruff voice responded from the back of the room. "How the heck do I know where my blood pressure will be 10 years from now?" I walked over to the blackboard and erased health from their vision statement. I said, "Oh, I guess this isn't very important, then." They reiterated that it was the most important item on the list. I asked them why they could tell me where they would be financially in 10 years, but they could not tell me where their health would be. They were not setting goals around personal health and well-being, despite the fact that it was the most important factor in their vision of the future.

Goals should be multilevel and multidimensional. People

are motivated more by goals that are difficult to reach than by simply "doing their best." If I have a one-dimensional goal to earn $1 million in two years and I don't reach that goal, I have left myself wide open to feeling like a failure. Your goal should include a whole range of other factors: how you carry out your plan, other aspects of your personal world, and so on. I tell athletes that on any given day, there should be at least 10 things on their checklist. The object is to check off at least seven or eight of the items every single day. One point may be how they react to the negative things that they face in their environment. Another might be related to "stick-to-it-iveness."

When you get involved in setting your own vision and aligning your goals with that vision, you acquire one other powerful ally—commitment. I have never met a person who is fully committed to someone else's goals. If you have quotas or guidelines that have been set for you by an employer, take ownership of them and rewrite them to coincide with your own life vision. We are the product of three things, said Viktor Frankl in his landmark book, *Man's Search for Meaning:* heredity, environment, and our own decisions.

Imagery and visioneering

It's not enough to define a vision and align clear-cut, well-defined goals with it. It is essential that you communicate that vision and those goals to yourself. Your body does not communicate in French, German, English, Russian, Italian, or Portuguese: your body speaks imagery. Imagery is the language that will lodge the vision deep within the core of your being, so that it pulls you, day after day, relentlessly toward itself. Seeing yourself on a daily basis making a difference, getting in touch with your goals, achieving and celebrating milestones brings precision to the day-to-day process of incorporating vision into your world.

This chapter was entitled Visioneering to convey the idea of taking a vision and applying the skills of engineering to it.

One outgrowth of visioneering is direction. Having a beacon—a vision—to guide you, then setting day-to-day goals
that lead you down the well-lit path of that vision, gives you
a clear sense of purpose and direction in life. The process
doesn't necessarily mean making massive changes, by the
way. Indeed, often a small goal, 10 years down the road, is
seen as the trim-tab adjustment that led to a major change.

I hadn't seen a friend who is in the investment business
for five years, and I was surprised at his fitness level and
general glow. He had run a marathon and had just returned
from a mountain-climbing trip. Five years earlier that would
have been totally unthinkable, considering his overall fitness level at that time, the development of which had been
impeded by his (over)work schedule. I said, "Terry, how did
you make such dramatic changes in your life?"

"Whole wheat bread," he replied.

"Right," I said, laughing, "whole wheat bread."

"No, truthfully whole wheat bread. My wife, Bonnie, said
to me, 'look, why are we buying white bread and dark
bread? Why can't you eat the dark bread that I bring into
the house?' She showed me several articles that clearly outlined how superior whole wheat bread was, and so it just
made sense. But I agreed only to eat whole wheat bread. I
didn't agree to any other change. Yet five years later I am on
a whole different dietary track. I'm running, swimming,
cycling, and getting a lot more out of my life. But it started
with one small change."

A Gallup poll published in *American Health* magazine in
1990 reported:

- Positive feelings, not fear or self-disgust, are what motivate most people to change.
- People are about 10 times likelier to change on their own
  (30 percent) than in working with a doctor (3 percent) or
  psychologist (less than 3 percent).
- A sudden flash of insight or an unexpected event is likelier to push someone to action than a carefully developed
  plan.

- Spontaneity is often the rule. In 51 percent of the cases, people just did it.
- One step at a time does it: 75 percent began on a day-to-day basis.

Visioneering involves three distinct phases: vision—inventing your future; decision—deciding on goals and making a commitment to action; precision—aligning daily activities with goals and vision.

The day-to-day of visioneering

The day-to-day can be monitored by asking ourselves simple questions. "Is this the best use of my time right now?" "Is this the best use of my life right now?" When looking for drive or energy to make a change, ask yourself, "Do I love X more than I dislike Y?" For example, "Do I love health more than I dislike disease?" "Do I love having financial resources more than I dislike having to be frugal?" "Do I love being open-minded more than I hate being pigheaded?" Mastery over your life comes from mental dedication to the enrichment of everyday life.

It's equally important to ask: "How does what I am doing right now fit in with my vision?" Visioneering is the process of opening up ourselves to the big questions and devising plans to get us there, much like going from the narrow-internal attentional focus to the broad-external. At the center of the process is a deep-seated trust in yourself and in the right thing happening as you go about your quest. Successful visioneering results from a profound shift in your inner equilibrium but this shift comes from doing small things. Feelings of receptivity and equanimity replace things to worry about, but life's obstacles suddenly don't appear as formidable when we see them in relation to our larger personal vision and goals. The challenge of the search is to move beyond what others expect of you to what is most meaningful for you. As Henry James said: "Live all you can;

it's a mistake not to. It doesn't so much matter what you do in particular, so long as you have had your life. If you haven't had that, what have you had?"

CHAPTER TEN

Mental Preparation

The important thing is this: to be able at
any moment to sacrifice what we are for
what we could become.
—Charles Du Bos

Great, consistent performances do not occur by accident; they are the result of careful mental and physical preparation. Dr. Terry Parsons, of Bowling Green State University in Ohio, did a thorough study of the characteristics of elite athletes, psychologically, sociologically, and physically. He found that any special advantage that elite athletes possessed was, in his opinion, primarily psychological. In his interviews with Olympic athletes, sports psychologist Terry Orlick found that some of his subjects felt their self-taught mental preparation process could have been shortened if they had had adequate instruction in this area. Likewise in business. Research done by Dr. Martin Seligman, of the University of Pennsylvania, showed that in the insurance industry, optimism can be learned and can become a main feature to success, even when initial aptitude tests indicate a low probability of success for a particular person.

There is no question that thoughts influence performance. A hazy preparation leads to a hazy performance. Studies of stuntmen have shown that these high risk-takers tend to be positive and open-minded. They see themselves as risk eliminators, viewing everything as a challenge, not as a threat. Mental preparation is crucial to their success. Their key to mastery is their positive self-belief and their meticulous planning—physically and mentally. They increase their level of control through careful review of the event, visualizing the positive outcome. Then they work on emptying their minds before a stunt, developing a strong focus on the immediate task at hand, just as high-performance athletes do. (You may want to glance back at Michael Smith's profile in chapter two to refresh your memory of the way an athlete prepares for competition.)

We don't have to be stuntmen or athletes to realize a profit from mentally preparing for key tests. The corporate groups I work with constantly identify the mental dimension as being the differentiating factor between success or failure. The key is to develop a plan to ensure that in any performance situation you get out what you're capable of doing. You can ensure that when you walk into the performance arena you are sharp and on your game.

I asked a group of sales professionals what key situations they needed to mentally prepare for. Here's what they had to say:

- selling ideas when confronted with a negative attitude
- making cold calls
- dealing with rejection, handling the unhappy customer
- making presentations to large groups of highly intelligent people
- closing the sale and asking for the cheque
- planning for the interview with a new client
- selling after a "flop"
- dealing with low-productivity slumps

When I asked a group of corporate executives what situations they needed to mentally prepare for, their list was different:

- dealing with the former coordinator of the center I was recently put in charge of
- dealing with unclear situations because of lack of knowledge or skill, or lack of awareness of circumstances
- coping with information overload and time constraints
- trying to negotiate change with an individual or organization that won't compromise
- dealing with performance appraisals, areas for improvement, and corrective behavior
- coping with unreasonable demands
- explaining to the board of directors why revenues are below forecasts
- terminating employees

When I asked a group of middle managers, again the responses were different, because of the different situations they found themselves in:

- making presentations to corporate management when you know you only have one shot to sell your project
- giving and receiving performance appraisals
- telling senior management that they've got it wrong
- firing employees
- negotiating with other organizations to "win" concessions
- keeping Elmer in line (there's an "Elmer" in every office, isn't there?)
- playing in the club championship (this is what they really want to learn how to mentally prepare for)

Other groups cited dealing with expectations, dealing with failures, plateauing, making presentations, balancing home and work life, and performing surgery while under duress.

All of these situations can be mentally prepared for. We all face different situations, so rather than approach mental preparation from a situational perspective, let's look at it from a time perspective. There are some things we have to prepare for immediately, for which we need moment-to-moment skills that we can use instantly. This, if you will, is the equivalent of your daily interest savings account. In the second category are key events one or two months down the road. These include presentations, job interviews, speeches at weddings, and so on. This is your short-term guaranteed investment certificate, your 30-day note. The real return on your investment of mental preparation, however, is long-term health. This is your savings bond.

The mental-preparation checklist

Here is a checklist, based on the skill areas that we've covered so far, that will ensure that you are sharp and on your game when you enter the performance arena:

- **Create a mental strategy and execute it.**
  Develop and carry out your mental strategy. Do not focus on results.
  Do focus on your strategy. Focus only on what you can control, not what you can't control.
- **Use imagery and mental rehearsals.**
  See yourself performing perfectly, being in the right frame of mind.
  Do consistent run-throughs in your head.
- **Set daily goals.**
  Identify clear daily goals as you move toward the event.
- **Target your optimal level of arousal.**
  Know in advance your appropriate level of arousal on a scale of one to ten. If it's too high, find where you need to be to perform at your best. Practice getting to that state. Use relaxation techniques or tapes to learn to achieve the optimal level of arousal.
- **Use power self-talk and affirmations.**
  Repeat positive, affirmative statement about the way you

wish to perform. Use short specific phrases for maximum impact.

- **Practice quality, quality practice.**

  Perfect practice makes perfect. Do the right thing in your head first. Be as precise as possible.

- **Develop and follow a pre-event ritual.**

  Create your own way of self-organizing before a big event. Develop and follow your own pre-event ritual.

- **Run simulations.**

  Do complete run-throughs, preferably in the environment where the event will take place or in a similar environment. Imagine yourself there.

- **Make mental preparation part of your overall preparation.**

  As an individual or with a team, incorporate proper mental preparation into your rehearsal schedule.

Moment-to-moment skills

You have a past history, so why not use it to your advantage? Most people can easily identify the situations that regularly throw them off course: the types of personalities they encounter that irritate or distract them, the circumstances in which they get overloaded or frazzled. And we've all had success at dealing with difficult situations. By identifying potentially difficult situations, by looking at how we've previously handled them successfully, or by putting to use some of the material that we've covered to this point, we can begin to develop a set of quick, moment-to-moment inner skills that we can use to help us refocus and get back on course when we've been blown off.

But, as we discussed in the Attentional Skills chapter, we have to be aware that we have been blown off course. Active awareness is the key to truly managing the moment and learning to be a "now-ist." Catching yourself when things go wrong will enable you to refocus in the direction that you need to go.

Another of the numerous possible skills for moment-to-moment mastery is scenario performing, which we covered under Imagery. In an interview in *Golf Digest*, Johnny Miller described how he used scenario performing with great success to manage the difficult moments that he faced daily on the professional golf tour:

> My theory, when I was in my prime, was that I had three guys playing for me. I had three distinct swing images. I had Lee Trevino, where I opened up my left foot and took it back and leaned into my left foot and hit this low little squeeze fade. I had Tony Lema, where I took it outside, sort of like Hubert Green with a light grip, and dropped it in and hooked the ball high. And I had Johnny Miller, who hit the ball pretty straight.
>
> So no matter what pin or what hole it was, one of those three guys had the perfect shot for that hole. And I learned to play that way. The advantage of it was that I knew on every day one or two of those three guys was going to be playing well. No way that all three of them were going to be playing badly. The problem is now I see a lot of young players, they have one guy playing for them. They have one shot and one shot alone. If that one guy is having a bad day there is no fallback. People don't know it, but that was one of the keys to my success. I even talked to Trevino before I hit it. "C'mon, Lee, this is your shot."
>
> And it was so easy it was a piece of cake. When I had all three, I was tough. There was no pin that I couldn't go for. That feeling of confidence was like, "Hey, I have all the arrows in my quiver and every hole is no problem, John."

Scenario performing may not be your bag. Perhaps you'll develop an excellent breathing technique (centering), or the ability to immediately change perspective (reframing). Perhaps you'll use an image to allow you to let go of what's bothering you (releasing or parking). In any event, managing moment-to-moment requires the application of mental skills. But, once again, awareness is the key. By looking at situations carefully we can begin to see those events and people that are likely to blow us off course. We can then be prepared, if and when that happens, with a clear plan of what mental skills to use and how to use them.

Mental preparation for key or major events

When I talk about a major event, I'm referring to something you know is going to happen. You know when and where it will take place, who will be there, the sequence of events, and so on. It could be a speech, a confrontation that you know will occur, an important sales presentation, a tennis match, getting married, or a job interview.

Every mental-preparation plan for a key event is designed to do two things: 1. keep you confident and focused on the task; and 2. move you to the appropriate energy level and attentional focus to excel. In other words, to get you into the ideal state for how you want to feel and be in order to perform the event well. So the very first step is to ask yourself just that: If this were a fair and just world, how would I like to be and feel when I have finished, for instance, making a speech? Let's use making a speech as our example through this section.

If I have a clear idea of how I want to feel and act, then I can engage in mental activities that will move me toward that state. The key is to apply mental skills before critical points occur. In the athletic world, the runner has to apply her mental strategy before heavy fatigue sets in. In the business world, the presenter has to plan to apply his mental skills before difficult situations occur so that he is in a state that allows him to handle those difficult situations. Let's break this down into skills to be applied on the day of the big event, as well as an hour before, just before, and during the presentation.

The day of the presentation

First and foremost, bear in mind that dead time—time when nothing is planned and nothing is happening—can usually hurt your performance. That is to say, things that can hurt your performance can occur during those times when you haven't adequately planned what you are doing. Let's start at the beginning of the day when you wakeup, because your initial attitude can sometimes determine your perception of events for that day. How you wake up is your mood-set, and it often takes hours to get over negative things that have occurred subconsciously during the night while you were sleeping. You want to wake up happy and tolerant of frustrations. To wake up positively on a presentation day, wake up slowly, use positive self-talk, do some slow stretching, smile to yourself (remember a smile can change your blood chemistry). Some people put cue words by the bed to remind them to start thinking positively.

Many athletes will not get out of the bed until they feel that they are in an appropriate mood for competition. They'll take an extra two or three minutes to mentally replay a past successful performance, so that they get out of bed in the mood that they want to be in for their performance. They don't allow themselves to be victims of what might have occurred subconsciously during the night.

Generally, during the day of a performance, it's a good idea to design activity to avoid upsets. Stay away from activities that are varied, complex, or stressful and distract you from your speech. Your presentation is important and you want to perform at your optimum. The time before it is not the time for solving major life problems. Getting totally lost in matters irrelevant to the day's major task will remove your focus, and you will not be as sharp as you would like to be. Minor diversions are excellent where there is no risk of upset: games, cards, checklists, or small simple skills.

The key on the day of the event is to establish within yourself a "taking care of business" attitude. If, for example, you notice that you're worried about a particular section of the speech, simply stop, acknowledge that you have that sense of worry, and take care of it. Use a centering technique, rehearse that part of the speech (perhaps go somewhere where you can say it out loud), see the way you want the audience to respond, and so forth. You want to establish the mind-set that says: Got a problem? Take care of it!

These simple acts help create a sense of self-management and focus, but above all else, you must monitor and control your arousal level. It's true that many performances are blown because the performer is uptight at the moment, but a fair number are blown because by presentation time the person is fatigued, since she's been so pumped up and hyped all day. By the time the event arrives, her energy is spent, and she's flat and unmotivated in her presentation.

You can't afford to waste excessive amounts of energy during the day of the presentation. It is important that you be rested. If you find you can't rest, narrow your attentional focus on the performance and review it; rehearse it in a relaxed manner. The best way to rest is to use a relaxation procedure. If you find your arousal level getting too high, take some time to use either a miniature or a full relaxation technique. But don't do relaxation during the last hour and a half before your performance. It takes the body time to regain the energy level necessary for a high performance following an effective relaxation session.

Whether you spend a lot of time with other people depends entirely on you. Some people are relaxed and find they can ease their tension by not being alone; others are agitated or irritated by having people around them. You will know which is right for you. Don't put yourself in a situation where people around you manipulate you into going somewhere or doing something that you don't really want to do. Manage your energy.

If you experience a loss of confidence, this usually comes as a result of a change in your appraisal of the events. Again, relax and use some positive imagery. Simulate a part of the action. Provoke assertive or aggressive behavior in yourself. See yourself being strong and powerful. Use your mood words.

When you notice an increase in tension, this can either be anxiety or a precursor to anxiety. Again, divert yourself with some simple task that keeps you focused. Use relaxation with imagery. Sometimes physical activity—walking or stretching—will help. Above all else, do something to get perspective on the event. You have many facets to your life and many wonderful qualities, and this performance is just one of the thousands of things that you will do in your life. An infinite number of things are more important—your health, your loved ones—than this single event. Maintaining that perspective will allow you to perform successfully.

At site, an hour or so before the presentation
This is a time when performance can be drastically affected—positively or negatively. It's essential to maintain emotional and mental control for the task at hand. I'm a firm believer that this hour should be planned, not so rigidly that you become a robot, but carefully enough to move you into the exact state you want to be in.

First and foremost, familiarize yourself with the facility. Athletes walk around and find places where they can get personal space if necessary. Walk out to the performance arena and see your presentation from various angles. This, of course, applies not only to the presenter, but also to the person who's about to be a witness in a courtroom, or to anyone facing a major event. Where are the washrooms? Where can you concentrate on your own? Imagine how you're going to use that personal space.

Another part of the pre-performance ritual is a warm-up that's designed to produce the appropriate attentional focus and arousal level so that you achieve the feelings necessary for an ideal performance state. At this juncture, it's important not to depend on others. If you need equipment, make sure that it's there, unless you have someone you can really trust to take care of such details, so that technical concerns are not preying on your mind. The key thing is to be focused on what you're doing. If you're trying to get the slide projector setup, concentrate only on the slide projector. You don't want to establish the habit of doing one thing while focusing on another. The athlete, for example, who's doing his stretching and thinking about something else begins to establish the pattern of focusing on other things while performing. You want to be truly a "now-ist," focused exactly on what you are doing. Gradually move your arousal level to the appropriate level for your performance. When I'm giving an after-dinner speech, I always make sure that I have time between the end of dinner and the start of my talk to go out, walk the hallway, shake the cobwebs out, say some affirmations about being strong and powerful—all calculated to move myself to the state I want to be in. On the other hand, if you find, in that hallway, that your arousal level is too high, you can do something to bring it down. Mental preparation depends totally on you. So does mental rehearsal. At this point, some people like to rehearse some of their key points, which brings us to our next section.

Just before the presentation

In the last four or five minutes, you need to become narrow and focused on what you're doing. Get in touch with the very first thing you are going to say. Rehearse your opening joke or pitch. If you focus at this point on the long term, or on how you have to succeed, you are fixating on things that will not assist you. However, if you get a great early response from the audience, that will carry you through to the completion of your presentation.

Do whatever you can to build your confidence. Remind yourself that you've chosen to do this: assess your inner state and recognize that it's normal to feel nervous and anxious. Remind yourself that you're strong and focused on the task.

During the performance

In many ways, maintaining the ideal inner state during the performance is similar to keeping in touch with the "moment-to-moment" skills that we described at the start of this section. But there are several other techniques that help—for example, having the performance segmented so that at the end of each section you can remind yourself, "Good. Excellent. You're on track. That's one section done." Task-relevant content allows you to control and plan for the dead spots. Like an actor you need a carefully planned script.

During the performance, allow for several pauses. Pauses seem to last forever to a speaker, but to the audience they are simply a break that gives them time to digest what they've just heard. Use a pause to stay mentally strong by interjecting powerful mood words and task-relevant thoughts that will keep you at your optimum energy level. The key is to follow the script—and I am not talking about the speech you are giving—but rather your strategic script: make eye contact, project to the back of the room, shift your gaze from left to right, use your hands. When you are involved in carrying out your strategy, success just follows naturally.

It's nice, as well, to have a distraction plan to refocus and put you back on course if necessary. I'm reminded of the head of a large multinational corporation who frequently had to appear in court in investigations for discovery whenever the name of his company's franchise was being used inappropriately. He had the unfortunate attitude of absolutely hating and distrusting attorneys. Because of his inability to deal with lawyers, his arousal level increased to the point that he lost sight of his mission and strategy, and spouted too much information in a confrontational manner, with the result that he took four or five times as long in the courtroom as he would have liked.

We designed a simple mental-preparation plan for him. His oil light, the sign that he was off course, was to be his back. When he started to lean forward so that his back left contact with his chair, that was a signal that he was getting away from his strategy. His attentional strategy was to be "down and out"—that is, his arousal level was to be low, and his focus out. By maintaining this arousal level and focus, he was able to see where the questions were going, give only the information that was necessary, and appear to be open to what was happening, rather than defensive, pigheaded, and confrontational. Simply by using centering techniques when he noticed he was getting anxious, putting his back against the back of the chair, assuming an open posture, asking for a repeat of the question on occasion to buy a little time to relax, he was able to cut two thirds off the time that he spent in courtrooms.

Designing a mental preparation program

Responding to the questions that follow will help you decide the actual makeup of your personal mental preparation program. These questions cover all the skills that we have discussed and will help you to design a pre-event and during-event plan. Following these questions, we will cover some general rules of mental preparation, but I'll mention the most important principle here. Coaches refer to the KISS method, which stands for Keep It Simple, Stupid. Don't complicate it. Don't make it so complex that it becomes a distraction in and of itself. Adequate, simple mental preparation, combined with awareness, will move you to where you can perform consistently at high levels and be on your game all of the time.

Active awareness
* Am I aware of what I'm feeling and thinking, of my physiological state (my breathing, arousal level, etc.)?
* Am I aware of how these internal dynamics are affecting my external behavior, and vice versa?
* Can I disidentify—step back and take on the role of observer—so I can then make a decision that will keep me in control of my performance?

Positivism
* With what attitudes am I approaching important situations and events in my life?

- Am I committed—curious and involved—or am I alienated?
- Do I feel challenged or threatened?
- Do I have a sense of control—that I can make an impact— or do I feel powerless?
- What skills do I have at my disposal to act in a positive way?
- Can the event be reframed?
- Do I need to change what I say to myself?
- What affirmations can I develop to deal with this situation?

Attentional skills
- What are my attentional strengths?
- Where am I most likely to overload?
- What attentional style(s) is (are) required?
- Will I need to shift styles?
- What strategies can I implement to maintain the attentional style(s) and shifts required—behaviorally, environmentally, internally?

Energy management
- What arousal level is appropriate?
- Am I likely to be too high, too low, just right?
- If I need to boost my arousal level, how will I do that?
- What techniques for energizing can I use?
- If I need to bring my arousal level down, how will I do that? What strategies for relaxing, reducing tension or anxiety can I use?

Short-term strategies
- breathing techniques
- stretching techniques
- muscle-relaxing techniques
- imagery
- juggling and other absorbing activities
- my own personal techniques

Long-term energy management
- meditation
- audiotapes
- biofeedback
- progressive relaxation
- autogenic relaxation
- Zen, yoga, transcendental meditation
- tranquility tanks
- breathing techniques

Imagery
- Am I aware of what I "image in" during important moments?
- Have I tapped into my natural abilities for imaging?
- Am I consciously using this skill to assist me in my development and endeavors?
- How can I use imagery to assist me in a given situation?

Vision
- What is the purpose of _____in my life?
- What is my vision of myself in 10 years, 20 years?
- Can I describe it? Can I see it? Can I feel it? What am I shooting for in my life?
- What form of resistance may make it difficult for me to hold this vision—externally, internally?
- What can I do to assist myself in holding this vision? Can I make clear and specific goals for one year, six months, tomorrow, whatever length of time feels appropriate?
- Can I imagine myself accomplishing these goals?

These questions might suggest that the mental preparation process is complex; nothing could be further from the truth. If you analyze what you need, based on a past performance in the area for which you are preparing, it is a relatively simple process. For example, deciding if you need personal space, or if you're the kind of person who can be around others before an important performance, is one simple parameter to consider.

When I first started working with figure skater Brian Orser before he became world champion in 1987, we sat down and analyzed three successful performances and three performances in which he did not perform as well as he might have. We looked at what he did on the day of, and just before, those major skating competitions, and a clear pattern emerged. There were certain behaviors preceding the successful performances that were not there prior to the unsuccessful ones. For example, he went for a walk before going to the rink. That sounds insignificant, but when I asked him what he did on the walk, he told me that on the walk away from the hotel, he would be thinking of what had happened that day. Brian comes from a very large family, who were usually with him for big events, and lots of activity occurred. But, he said, when he turned around to walk back to the hotel, he came back as a skater. The minute he turned around, he focused his attention on what he was going to do when he got to the rink and how he was going to prepare, and he got in touch with the skating performance that he wanted to give. That walk performed an important psychological function for him.

Once you learn to use the skills outlined in this book, you begin to become unconsciously competent with them. (Remember the Active Awareness chapter.) You automatically take the time to get in touch with the mental skills that are important before performing.

Mental preparation becomes relatively simple. I encourage you to take the time to design a mental preparation plan that is simple, compact, and, above all, personal. Taking a few minutes before a performance to ensure that you are in the right mind-set. Great performances are not accidents; they come from careful preparation and excellent skills. With each success, great performances aren't just possible, they are probable.

Conclusion

Well, I hope you've enjoyed reading this book as much as I enjoyed writing it. As in any leave-taking, there are always a few more things to say, and ultimately I'm sure that there will be a few more things that I wish I'd said. So, in no particular order of importance, I'd like to leave you some thoughts that may assist you in becoming the high-level performer that you have within you.

1. You may ask yourself, "Do I really need this?" I think we all need to become aware of what goes on inside us and how it affects our outside performance. You not only need it, you deserve it. Be kind to yourself. Remember that being realistic is a learned skill.

2. Sometimes going inside and discovering what is going on there is hard work, but it's interesting work. If we take the time to get to know those around us, shouldn't we take the time to get to know ourselves and the impact that our interior and exterior realities have on our functioning and well-being?

3. Whenever insights strike you, when you've noticed things that you didn't know or notice before, make sure you write

them down. Don't let observations and inspirations that are important escape you. Hang on to them.

4. Please remember to take with you a sense of humor—life's best management tool.

5. And, most important, remember that your only task in any situation is to carry out your strategy. You cannot ensure the outcome. You could be blindingly brilliant in a sales presentation, yet the customer might choose to buy from her brother-in-law. Moreover, if you adjusted your strategy on the basis of that result, you might be moving from an effective strategy to one that would not work as well. Evaluate only how effectively you carry out your strategy. The elite swimmer sets a personal best, or even a world record, only to have it broken by somebody else in the race; he or she has no control over that. You cannot always control the result.

In 1988, Elizabeth Manley skated a brilliant performance and landed five triple jumps in her long program, yet she finished second. She couldn't control the judges, who put Katarina Witt and her three triple jumps first. I recall vividly the aftermath of that performance: Elizabeth and I were downtown celebrating at a home that had been rented for some of the coaches of the Canadian figure-skating team. We left there at about two o'clock in the morning to return to the Olympic village, where we had to go through security clearance and walk along the underground corridors of the village to get back to our quarters. We were in a tunnel with absolutely no one around, and Elizabeth was walking with her silver medal around her neck. Then ahead of us we saw two cleaners who were washing the floor. As we approached them, they silently slipped against the wall to let us by because the tunnel was so narrow. They didn't say a word. As we passed, they both broke into applause. They knew...they knew that Elizabeth had performed like a champion.

APPENDIX A

Relaxation

The script that follows is designed to help you make a tape that will teach you the skills of relaxation and positive self-talk (affirmations). If you like, you may have instrumental music that you find soothing playing in the background; this will not only enhance the relaxation exercise, but it will also help to cut out distractions such as traffic. Speak in a slow, relaxing tone. Whenever you see an ellipsis (...), pause for two or three seconds. This will allow for reflective time during the relaxation.

Affirmations are more powerful when you are very relaxed because, in a relaxed state, you are more receptive to suggestion. But remember, the suggestions you give yourself are of your own creation. Before starting the affirmation exercise, create affirmations for yourself that signify what it is you need at the moment. If, for example, you are working on confidence, write affirmations that have to do with confidence. If you are in need of "stick-to-it-ive-ness" or acceptance, then write affirmations related to those states. You may not choose to use five—as suggested in the Optional Affirmation Section of the script—you may use only one. It's entirely up to you. In the script I suggest some general affirmations. Whenever I suggest an affirmation, you are to follow by inserting one of your own. You can choose to use the general affirmations or to ignore them. If you don't want to use the affirmation section, leave it out and tape only the relaxation exercise.

Before beginning the tape, let's review the four steps that Dr. Herbert Benson outlined as necessary to elicit the "relaxation response":

1. Get into a comfortable position. You may sit or lie down. Make sure your back is supported and you can hold this position for 20 minutes without putting undue strain on your body.
2. Find a quiet environment where you will not be disturbed.
3. Choose a mental device—something to focus your attention on. Your tape will be the mental device in this instance.
4. Assume a passive attitude. This is very important. One cannot *try* to relax; one must *allow* relaxation to occur. Thoughts, doubts, and sounds, from both inside and outside, are bound to come along. If you choose to attend to each one, you will be distracted. Use those distractions as signs to deepen your concentration and return to your voice on the cassette.

When we start the exercise we engage in the centering technique for the first few minutes because we want to acquire that skill, as well. When we do, we place 100 percent of our attention on our diaphragm as we breathe in, then shift our attention to our shoulders, which will fall, and to our buttocks, which will sink, when we let the breath out.

This tape is just an exercise in relaxation with affirmations. It is a very simple exercise. Try not to be judgmental about the process. With practice you will become very good at it. (At points in the following script I use the second person— "you." I will say, for example, "You are becoming more and more relaxed." You can substitute "I" if you prefer to use the first person.)

The Script

Get into a comfortable position give yourself permission to relax. Let the music surround you...

Let's start with a centering exercise...I breathe out...and as I breathe in, I focus 100 percent of my attention on my diaphragm, which extends slightly...As I let the air out, I focus on my shoulders, which drop...and on my buttocks, which sink...I breathe in and allow my diaphragm to extend...I hold the breath for a second and shift my attention to my shoulders, which fall...and to my buttocks which sink...Try three or four deep breaths on your own now...slowly and evenly...focusing 100 percent of your attention on your diaphragm and then shifting it to your shoulders and buttocks...

(Leave 30 seconds.)

Continue breathing deeply...and imagine the path that the air takes as it travels into your lungs...and hold that breath for a second...Then imagine the path that the air takes as it leaves...And I breathe in slowly to the count of one...and I hold my breath for a brief moment, becoming aware of that stillness...Then I slowly let the air out to the count of two...Now I breathe in slowly to the count of one, two, three, four,...and I breathe out slowly to the count of one, two, three, four, five, six, seven, eight...and I breathe in slowly to the count of four...and let it out slowly to the count of eight...That's excellent...

Now I want you to become aware of your left calf muscle...Focus all your attention on the left calf muscle...Be aware of its points of contact with the surface beneath you...Feel where it touches the surface...Imagine that it is getting heavy...and it is heavy...I imagine that it sinks slowly into the surface beneath me...becoming heavier and heavier...And I become aware of my right calf muscle...I place all my attention on that muscle...I become that muscle...and just let go...and imagine that it becomes warm and heavy...warm and heavy...

Become aware of your left thigh...Feel where it contacts the surface beneath you...Just let it go...Let it sink...I become totally aware of my left thigh muscle...I imagine its points of contact with the surface beneath me...I become aware of those points and I just let it go...Good...

Become aware of your right thigh muscle...and imagine where it's touching the floor, or the bed, or the chair beneath...Imagine that it becomes warm and heavy and sinks slowly...And once more I become aware of that right calf and thigh...I imagine that they are warm and heavy...I just let them sink and they do...

Become aware of your buttocks and where they are contacting the surface beneath them...Just let them go...Let them sink...I become aware of my breathing...I feel my stomach rise as I breathe in...and as the air leaves, it takes with it all the tension...my stomach gently falls...Good...

...If your mind has wandered, gently bring it back...Focus on my words...And my right leg is heavy...My right leg is heavy and warm...My left leg is becoming heavier and heavier...and warmer and warmer...

And as I breathe in, I feel my chest rise and I feel my rib cage expand...and I hold the breath for just a second, becoming aware of that tension...and then I let it go...and my rib cage falls...and the air takes with it all the tension from my body...

Become aware of your shoulder blades...and where they are contacting the surface beneath you...And I imagine that there are tiny strings gently pulling my shoulders back and allowing them to sink softly down...And I become aware of my shoulders...I imagine their points of contact...and I just let them go...And my body is becoming heavy and warm...relaxed and comfortable...but my mind is alert...my heartbeat is calm and regular...and I'm becoming more and more relaxed as my body breathes freely and comfortably...

Place all your attention on your forehead...Imagine your hairline...Just let it go...And it relaxes...Once more I place all my attention on my forehead...and I just let it go... Good...

Become aware of your jaw muscles...Just let them go...Let your mouth gently fall open...Imagine that you breathe down into your left arm...all the way into your fingertips...Feel the slight tingling sensation in your fingertips...the warmth...As you breathe out, imagine pulling up that sensation like a glove over your wrist and your forearm...over your elbow...over your bicep and tricep...Your left arm is heavy and relaxed...I become aware of the difference between my left and my right arm...so I breathe down into that right arm and I imagine the breath flowing all the way through to the fingertips...I feel that tingling, warm sensation in my fingertips...As I exhale, I pull that sensation like a glove...over my wrist and forearm and elbow and upper arm...and I imagine that my right arm is heavy and relaxed...And it is...

Imagine that you are walking...and ahead of you is an elevator...an elevator that will take you down to deeper and deeper levels of relaxation...This elevator has a glass panel in its backwall...and through it you can see, or imagine that you can see, a red number seven...And as you get comfortable in this elevator...it is luxurious and restful...the elevator starts slowly down...taking you to deeper and deeper levels of relaxation...past an orange-colored six...sinking deeper and deeper...past a yellow-colored five...becoming heavier and heavier...more and more relaxed...past a green four...sinking deeper and deeper past a blue three...down, down past a purple-colored two...As my elevator arrives gently at a violet-colored one...it slowly stops...

And I get off my elevator and ahead of me is my own mental training room...This is your room...You may decorate this room any way you wish...Ahead of you is a screen...a screen that you will be able to use to see things on at a later date...And there is a chair in that room that fits your body perfectly...

Sit in that chair now and feel how comfortable it is...And you are relaxed and sitting in your own mental training room...but your mind is alert...Your body is relaxed, but your mind is alert.

And above you, you can see a golden globe of energy...just a ball of energy...arm's-length above you, like a giant sun...As you pull down that ball of energy over your body it massages the tension out of your face...your neck and shoulders gently relax even further...pull it down over your chest and your stomach...over your hips...Feel its gentle rays massaging the tension out of your thighs...down over your knees and calves...

And you are extremely relaxed, lying in your mental training room...This is your room...You may come here at any time to see things as you want them to be...

Optional affirmation section

You may record any or all of these affirmations or create your own followed by a five- to ten-second pause. When you are actually doing the relaxation exercise, you can insert affirmations specific to what you need that day after each of these permanently recorded affirmations. This allows the exercise to stay current and adjust to your changing needs. State these affirmations clearly, strongly, and with feeling. I am now going to use some positive affirmations...

I have a clear sense of direction and purpose...Now repeat yours (leave five seconds on your tape)...

I act with confidence (leave five seconds on your tape)...

I accept the challenge of difficult situations (leave five seconds on your tape)...

I am creative and open to new ideas (leave five seconds on your tape)...

I am a winner, in every sense of the word. I am a winner (leave five seconds on your tape)...

As you lie here in your mental training room, feel how it feels to be this confident person...this competent person...This is who you are deep down inside...and the more that you practice and rehearse these affirmations, the more you bring this person and these skills into everyday life...(End of optional section.)

(Tape script continued)

You are relaxed and sitting in a comfortable chair in your mental training room...You have allowed yourself to relax by giving yourself permission to follow the simple steps that you will practice and that will become critical skills for you...In a minute you will leave your mental training room, but just look around and see this place...and remember that it is your place...that you can come here anytime you wish to see things as you want them to be...to find some peace and quiet...

Now you get up from your chair and walk to the door of your room...and look back...As you turn around you see ahead of you the elevator that will take you to higher and higher levels of awareness...As you move onto the elevator it starts to take you up...One...moving on up, becoming a little more alert...Two...on up...you are beginning to feel yourself coming out of this deep relaxation...Three...becoming more and more awake...And at four, I start to move my fingers around just a little bit...And at five, I become a little more alert...And at six, gently rocking just a little bit from side to side...And at seven, before I open my eyes, I slowly take two big, deep breaths...and as I let the air out the second time, I gently open my eyes...

(End of tape)

APPENDIX B

Imagery Exercise

The purpose of this tape is not only to achieve a deep, relaxed state, but also, while in that state, to use imagery to improve your performance in whatever area that you wish to pursue. Before using this tape, write down one or two skills that you would like to practice. They might be skills from your golf game, your presentation skills, or a new way of dealing with a difficult situation at work or at home. Before using the tape each time, decide which skill(s) you would like to mentally rehearse. The script suggests that you rehearse two skills, but you can choose to rehearse only one, if you wish. Again, if you prefer, you can change the word "you" to "I", or vice versa, as you record the tape. Remember to speak slowly and pause whenever you see an ellipsis (...). I have left a 30-second pause for each rehearsal. If the skill or action you would like to rehearse takes more time, leave a longer gap.

The Script

Get yourself in a comfortable position in a place where you know you won't be disturbed for a while...Give yourself permission to relax...Follow my words as you go through the program, keeping an open mind...Suspend judgement...Just allow it to happen...

Close your eyes and let your arms rest comfortably beside your body...Let your legs lie slightly apart so that the muscles can relax...Breathe in slowly to the count of four...and hold that breath just for a second, and let it go...And I breathe in slowly to the count of four...and I hold it for just a second, becoming aware of that soft spot where I hold the air...then I let it go to the count of eight...Take a moment now to practice that meditative, relaxing breathing...Four on the way in and eight on the way out...

(Pause for 30 seconds.)

Finish what you were doing...Let your body breathe for you...and notice the feelings of heaviness and warmth that come with relaxation...Become aware of your left leg...and imagine that the air moves down into that leg as you breathe...and as the air leaves, it takes with it any tension...and your left leg becomes heavy...I breathe slowly down into my left leg...and as I breathe out, the air gently leaves, taking with it all the tension, and my leg relaxes...

And I breathe slowly down into my right leg...I imagine the path the air takes as it leaves...taking with it any tension...and my right leg becomes warm and heavy...warm and heavy...

Become aware of your buttocks and where they are contacting the floor or chair...Just let them go...Feel the points of contact that your buttocks make with the surface beneath you...Just let go...That's it...Good...

I breathe in and my rib cage expands...As I exhale my ribs fall gently...I become more and more relaxed...With each exhalation, my body relaxes more and more...

Become aware of your forehead and just let it go...Become aware of your shoulder blades...Just let them fall...Good...If you hear any noises or distractions, use them to deepen your focus and concentration...I'm becoming more and more relaxed...but my mind is alert...My body is becoming more and more relaxed...but my mind is alert...

Become aware of your right shoulder blade and your left shoulder blade...and let them fall backwards gently...And

*breathe down into your right arm, all the way into your fin-
gertips...And feel that tingling sensation in your fingertips...and allow it to move up over your wrist and arm...up
over your shoulders and then down your body...Become
aware of your left arm and your fingertips...Feel that sensation, that tingling sensation...Pull up that sensation over your
wrist and your elbow and your arm...Let it run all down your
body, relaxing you...And your arms sink slowly and become
very, very heavy...*

*Feel the stillness within you...Try to locate your heart
rate...Feel it slow down as you relax...deeper and deeper,
slowing its pace...sinking into a state of relaxation and rest-
fulness...*

*Imagine a relaxing scene...Feel a gentle breeze...Visualize
a beautiful beach...or a sailboat...soft green grass...Beginning
at the top of your head, slowly scan your body...Check your
forehead and your jaw muscles...Any points of tension that
you find, just let them go...Check your shoulders and your
biceps and your forearms...your chest and your
stomach...your hips...your buttocks...your thighs...
knees...calves...and your feet...You are becoming more and
more relaxed...but your mind is alert...*

*You are standing at the top of an escalator, a staircase, or
an elevator...any device that you wish to take you down...and
this device will take you down to your mental-training
room...As you descend, you will become heavier and heavier...and more and more relaxed...*

*Off to the side, you can see a red number seven as you
slowly start to go down in the elevator...deeper and deeper...heavier and heavier...sinking down past an orange-colored six...becoming more and more relaxed...more and more
comfortable...past a yellow five...sinking down...down...down...past a
green-colored four...more and more relaxed...heavy...soft...calm...a blue
three...sinking down...gently...softly...past a purple-colored
two...down...down...slowly as you arrive at a violet-colored one...*

*Ahead of you is your mental training room...your place...Go
in and look around...See this room...See the way you have*

decorated it...the colors...the light...See the fresh flowers that you have put there...Smell their scent...Good...Look around that room and see your comfortable chair...and as you sit in it, feel it accept your weight...Feel yourself sink slowly into that chair...

You are relaxed and comfortable in your mental training room...and you can see ahead of you a large screen, upon which you will be able to imagine yourself performing...And on the screen, slowly coming into focus, is an image of you...You can see yourself...You can see a situation that you have decided to rehearse...Imagine yourself now practicing every detail with perfection...See the skill as you work on it...Feel what it feels like to be this performer...Take a few moments now and practice the first skill that you would like to reinforce...

(Pause for 30 seconds.)

Finish what you are doing...Good...Good...Feel how that feels...Hear the sounds that you would hear at this point...Smell the smells that might exist in that environment...Go back and replay it again...this time trying to use all the senses...

(Pause for 30 seconds.)

Good...That's excellent...Just get in touch with how good it feels to perform that skill so well...and know that you can practice this way and that you will get better and better...Believe that...Know that it is true...

Let's take the second skill now, but before you practice the skill, create the environment in which you will use this skill...See that environment...Hear the sounds that you would hear there...the colors...the smells...You are feeling confident...You are solid...and you are ready...Go ahead now and perform...in every detail, perform...

(Pause for 30 seconds.)

Now let's see it from another angle. Go ahead, perform the skill one more time, watching yourself from either a closer or greater distance, or looking out your eyes, as if you were inside your body at this moment, and see how it feels...Or think about performing the skill as if you were inside your body...Go ahead...just replay it...

(Pause for 30 seconds.)

Just finish what you are doing...Yes...And you are feeling strong and positive...yet relaxed and calm...performing skills as beautifully as you can perform them...

And you are sitting in your mental training room, very relaxed...mentally rehearsing skills that will help you perform at your best...In a moment you will come out of this mental training room and you will feel calm and alert and rested...but know that you can come here anytime to practice these skills...Know that you can improve your use of these skills in your everyday life by reinforcing them here...This is a laboratory where you can work on new ways of approaching difficult problems...

And now we will start to slowly move up and out of this deeply relaxed state...And we will move up, the way a bubble moves to the surface of a lake...gently and slowly...At one, I become a little more alert...slowly feeling my elevator gently taking me up...to a level two and on...moving up to level three...becoming more alert...a little more aware as I move up to a four...At five I gently move my fingers and toes...and at a six stretch very slightly...And at a seven, before I open my eyes, I take a couple of deep breaths.

(End of tape)

Notes

Page numbers on which cited material appear are shown in bold face.

Introduction
4. John Welch quoted in "Today's Leaders Look to Tomorrow," *Fortune* 121 (March 26, 1990): 58.

Chapter One
12. Ingemar Stenmark quoted in a conversation between the author and a Swedish coach.

Chapter Two
14. Gaetan Boucher in conversation with the author.

Chapter Three
37. Kurt Browning in conversation with the author.
39. Gaetan Boucher in conversation with the author.
39. Louis Wirth in preface to *Ideology and Utopia,* Karl Mannheim (New York: Harcourt, Brace and World, 1936), xii.

Chapter Five
76. See Herbert Benson, *The Relaxation Response* (New York: Avon, 1975).

Chapter Six
87. Steve Podborski in conversation with the author.
96. See Cal Botteril, "Energizing," *SPORTS: Science Periodical on Research and Technology In Sport.* 4 (December 1986): 1-6

Chapter Seven

102. Frank Schubert, *Psychology From Start to Finish* (Toronto: Sports Books Publisher, 1986), 118.

106. Linda Thom in "Concentrating When it Counts," *Coaching Review* 9 (January-February 1986): 23.

107. Ibid.

108. Ibid., 23.

108. Ibid., 24.

108. Ibid.

Chapter Eight

118. H.A. Overstreet, *The Mature Mind* (New York: Norton, 1959), 66.

119. Jean Decety and David Ingvar, "Brain Structures Participating in Mental Simulation of Motor Behavior: A Neuropsychological Interpretation," *Acta Psychologica* 73 (1990): 13.

125. Sylvie Bernier quoted in Terry Orlick and John Partington, *Psyched! Inner Views of Winning* (Ottawa: Coaching Association of Canada, 1986), 22-23.

Chapter Ten

165. Johnny Miller quoted in an interview in *Golf Digest* May 1991: 104.

Bibliography
and Suggested Reading

Assagioli, Roberto. *Psychosynthesis.* New York: Viking, 1972.

Benson, Herbert. *The Relaxation Response.* New York: Avon, 1975.

Botterill, Cal. "Energizing." *SPORTS: Science Periodical on Research and Technology in Sport.* 4 (December 1986): 1-6.

Borysenko, J. *Minding the Body, Mending the Mind.* Reading: Addison Wesley, 1987.

Campbell, Joseph. *The Hero's Journey.* San Franscisco: Harper and Row, 1990.

Carrington, Patricia. *Releasing.* New York: William Morrow, 1984.

Cooper, R. *The Performance Edge.* Boston: Houghton-Mifflin, 1991.

Cousins, N. *Head First: The Biology of Hope.* New York: E.P. Dutton, 1989.

Cousins, N. *The Healing Heart.* New York: Weatherhill, 1983.

Covey, S. *Seven Habits of Highly Effective People.* New York: Fireside, 1989.

Diaz, J. "Johhny Miller." *Golf Digest.* May 1991: 102-117.

Dogen, and Uchiyama, K. *Refining Your Life.* New York: Weatherhill, 1983.

Dossey, L. *Space, Time and Medicine.* Boston: New Science Library, 1982.

Fanning, P. *Visualization For Change.* Oakland: New Harbinger, 1988.

Frankl, V. *Man's Search For Meaning: An Introduction to Logotherapy.* Boston: Beacon Press, 1962.

Garfield, C. *Peak Performance: Mental Training Techniques.* Los Angeles: J.P. Tarcher, 1988.

Grigori, R. *Red Gold.* Los Angeles: J.P. Tarcher, 1988.

Handy, Charles. *The Age of Reason.* Boston: Harvard Business School Press, 1989.

Harp, David. *The Three-Minute Meditator.* Middlesex, Vermont: Musical Idiot, 1988.

Helmstetter, S. *What to Say When You Talk To Yourself.* Scotsdale: Grindle Press, 1986.

Justice, B. *Who Gets Sick?* Los Angeles: J.P. Tarcher, 1988.

LeShan, Lawrence. *You Can Fight For Your Life: Emotional Factors in the Causation of Cancer.* New York: M. Evans, 1977.

Loeher, J. *Mental Toughness Training For Sports.* Lexington, Mass.: Stephen Greene Press, 1986.

Loudis, L. et al. *Skiing Out of Your Mind.* Champaign, Ill.: Leisure Press, 1986.

Maddi, S. and Kobasa, S. *The Hardy Executive: Health Under Stress.* Homewood, Ill.: Dow-Jones-Irwin, 1984.

McCluggage, D. *The Centered Skier.* Toronto: Bantam, 1983.

Miller, S. *Performing Under Pressure.* Toronto: McGraw-Hill, 1992.

Newman, S. "Concentrating When It Counts." *Coaching Review.* 9 (January-February 1986) 22-25.

Nhat Hanh, Thich. *Peace is Every Step.* New York: Bantam, 1991.

Nideffer, R. *Athlete's Guide to Mental Training.* Champaign: Human Kinetics, 1985.

Orlick, T. and Partingtone, J. *Psyched! Inner Views of Winning.* Ottawa: Coaching Association of Canada, 1986.

Orlick, T. *Psyching for Sport.* Champaign: Leisure Press, 1986.

Overstreet, H.A. *The Mature Mind.* New York: Norton, 1959.

Pennington, S. *Healing Yourself.* Toronto: McGraw-Hill, 1988.

Schubert, Frank. *Psychology From Start to Finish.* Toronto: Sports Books Publisher, 1986.

Seligman, M. *Helplessness: On Depression, Development and Death.* New York: Freeman, 1975.

Seligman, M. *Learned Optimism.* New York: Knoph, 1990.

Seuss, Dr. *Oh, the Places You'll Go.* New York: Random House, 1990.

Siegel, B. *Love, Medicine and Miracles.* New York: Harper and Row, 1986.

July 19th, 9090